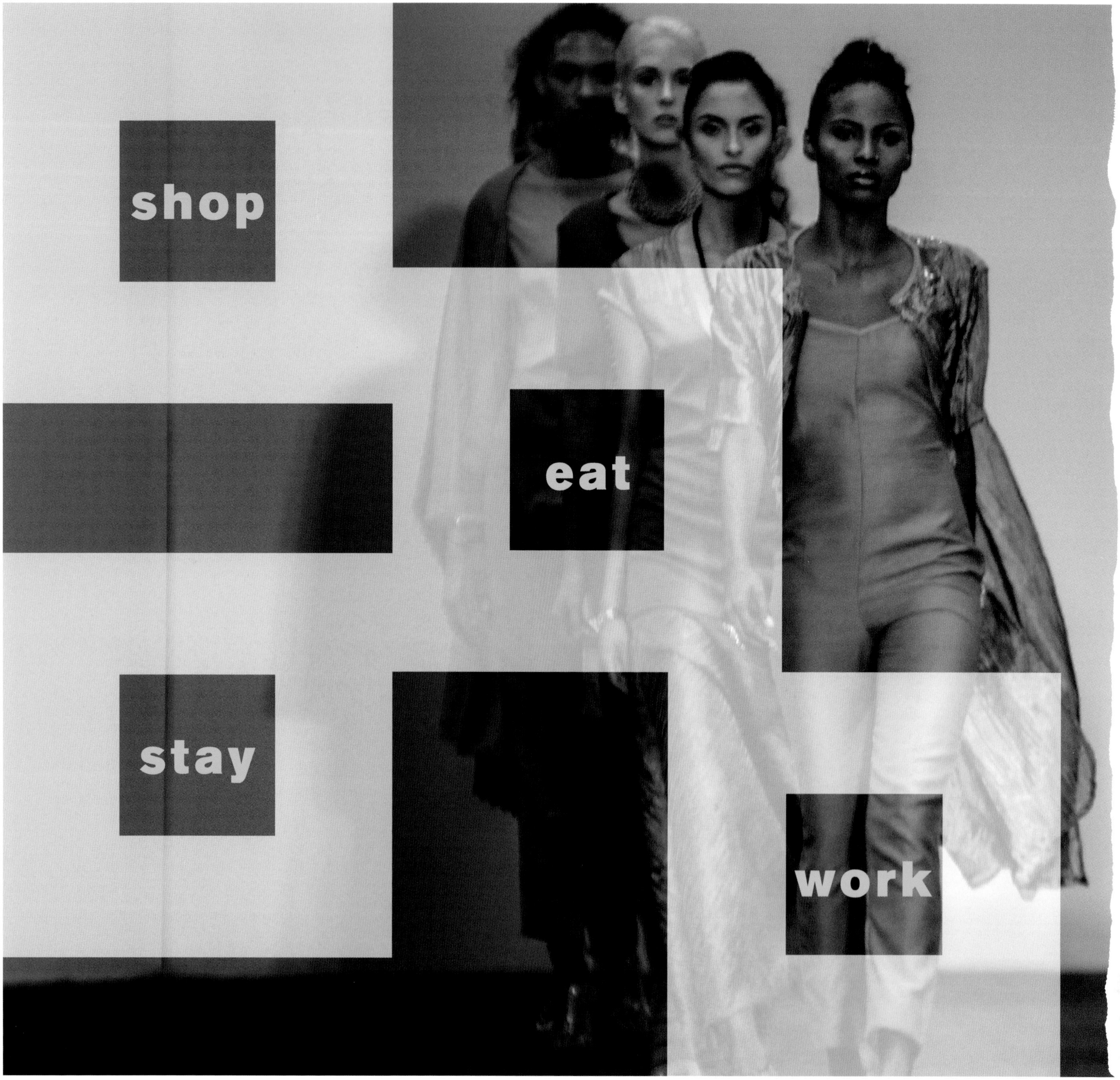
shop
eat
stay
work

WELCOME

A DTLA MOMENT

Great cities have great moments. Paris in the 1920s, London in the 1960s, Berlin in the 1990s...

...Downtown Los Angeles in the 2010s? We think so. It's difficult to recognize the essence of an era as it happens, but from street level in DTLA it looks like the stars are aligned for our big moment. In bars and restaurants, stores and galleries, concert halls and theaters, lofts and creative offices the excitement is infectious. So much is going on that it's hard to keep up.

Watching all this, we decided to put together this book to share what's happening. We soon realized that a great moment is defined by the people who create it, which is why many of the stories we're bringing you feature individuals living and working in DTLA. It may seem like a random collection of creative minds, but we do believe it represents the emerging spirit of Downtown.

When were the seeds for the DTLA renaissance sowed? Was it when a band of creatives started moving into a deserted, low-rent warehouse area by the river? When Frank Gehry redefined with a few brushstrokes what a concert hall could look like? When a bookstore claiming to be "the last" opened its doors? When a philanthropic couple decided to build a museum to share their vast art collection with the world? Or was it when community members got together to seek solutions to the homeless problem? The stories in this book contemplate these questions and take a look at the forces driving the dynamic changes taking place in the city.

We hope these pages will give you an idea about our neighborhood and some understanding for our excitement. But most of all, we hope that our stories will make you put the book down and go out and experience DTLA for yourself.

CONTENTS

Vol. 01 // 2017

COVER

Original art created
by Tommii Lim for
DISTRICT BOOK//DTLA.
See page 48

Welcome

Downtown

30
STYLE SQUAD

126

158

118

5 ESSENTIAL RULES FOR FULLY ENJOYING DTLA

RULE NO. 1

WALK IT!

Welcome to the most walkable neighborhood in L.A.

By Elizabeth Turner // Photography by Maximilian Rivera

At the heart of a city designed around car culture, Downtown Los Angeles stands out as a walker's paradise. Boasting a walk score of 94, this patchwork of urban neighborhoods offers a sidewalk-level view of the rich history and dynamic future of Los Angeles living. For Downtown residents—the number of which has more than tripled since the revitalization boom kicked off in 1999—DTLA is the antidote to L.A. gridlock. According to a 2015 survey by the Downtown Center Business Improvement District, 22 percent of locals live and work here, and 62 percent of that group walk to work every day. Errands are easy to accomplish on foot. And with the city's mass transit system centered Downtown, many residents live happily car-free.

A longtime stomping ground for artists, DTLA is dense with museums, galleries, theaters and other performance spaces. New shops, restaurants and bars pop up every week, inviting residents and visitors to hit the streets in search of the next great thing.

Model Genevieve Abell (Aston Models) wears fashions by DTLA-based Paper Machine. Read more about Paper Machine designer Natashia Miyazaki in "My Day: Fashion District" on page 98. Styling by Shari St. Jones; makeup by Christine Tirado; hair by Yumi Kotani.

A MAJOR CROSSROADS
In 1924, more than half a million people a day crossed the intersection of 7th Street and Broadway, making it the world's busiest intersection of the time. To see the evolution of this historic crossroads, turn to page 56.

EAT, DRINK, REPEAT

So many flavors, so little time.

The best of L.A.'s vibrant food scene is on fine display in DTLA. High and low options abound, from taco stands and gourmet food trucks to rooftop bars serving craft cocktails with big city views. Splurge-worthy dining spots include Neal Fraser's Redbird, situated in the former rectory of Vibiana Cathedral, and Otium at The Broad museum. Rolling with a crew that just can't decide? Head straight to historic Grand Central Market, a foodie-approved food court where anyone can find his or her heart's desire.

Genevieve samples the strawberry sorbet from Gelateria Uli's splendid selection of small-batch frozen treats. Necklace, crystal ring and off-the-shoulder Alexa romper, all by Paper Machine. Watch by Komono.

GELATERIA ULI
Spring Arcade Building, 541 S. Spring St., Historic Core
213-900-4717 // gelateriauli.com

MINGLE!

*Say hello to local dogs
(and their humans).*

DTLA is dog-friendly by design.
When the 1999 Adaptive Reuse
Ordinance spurred the conversion
of commercial buildings into
lofts, landlords actively courted
dog lovers with pet-friendly
policies and amenities. Canine
companions got residents walking
the streets and talking to their
neighbors. Join the conversation:
Enthusiastic locals know the best
spots to explore.

**Babak Housh, owner of Cleaners LA,
dry cleaning and tailoring studio,
and his friend Suzzi Stardust take
a play break with their bull terrier
rescue pups, Axel and Simone.**

CLEANERS LA
314 E. 8th St., Fashion District // 213-910-2522

RULE
NO. 4

FOLLOW THE ART

Explore the cultural scene.

With world-class museums (The Broad, MOCA), the galleries of the Arts District and Gallery Row, and head-turning murals around every corner, the visual art vibe is strong in DTLA. For music, theater and dance, fans flock to epic venues such as Walt Disney Concert Hall, The Music Center and the historic Ace Theatre.

MURAL ART BY PETER GRECO AT AMERICAN HOTEL
303 S. Hewitt St., Arts District // 213-545-4695 // americanhotella.com

TIME TRAVEL

Feel the history.

Arguably the most beautiful thing about DTLA is its palpable sense of the city's rich history. Architectural gems include The Bradbury Building at left (1893), with its skylit atrium, cage elevators and Victorian ironwork. The Biltmore Hotel (1923) harks back to the glamorous 1920s, when Broadway was the epicenter of L.A. shopping and nightlife. A few blocks away, the Romanesque Fine Arts Building (1926) originated as a swanky studio/ gallery space for Downtown artists, but became an office building during the Great Depression. And don't miss what is still considered one of the last great train stations: Union Station (1939), a gorgeous mash-up of Art Deco and Mission Revival styles.

THE BRADBURY BUILDING
304 S. Broadway, Historic Core

SILVER SCREEN REDUX

DTLA's historic Theater District is making a comeback—70 years after its big breakout.

By Lydia Mack

O n a stretch of Broadway that was once littered with heaps of last night's empty bottles and flattened cigarette butts, tourists and hipsters cross paths at the trendy Ace Hotel, housed alongside the iconic United Artists Theatre. A block and a half away, a new marquee shines brightly at the Globe Theatre. Just up the street is the Orpheum Theatre, where plenty of young hopefuls have chased the dream at *American Idol* auditions.

Broadway's stretch of 12 movie palaces in six blocks makes up the Broadway Theater District. By its heyday in 1931, the district had the highest concentration of cinemas in the world, with seating capacity for more than 15,000 patrons.

But after hitting its peak in the 1930s, the Theater District went dark. Architectural masterpieces were buried under wholesale jewelry stores, swap meets and discount electronics. Most auditoriums went decades without seeing people and instead were used for storage. The few theaters lucky enough to make use of their seats were those leased by Spanish-speaking movie venues and churches. But thanks to City Councilman José Huizar's "Bring Back Broadway," the Los Angeles Conservancy, the Broadway Theatre Group and the Los Angeles Historic Theatre Foundation, the Theater District is enjoying its moment in the spotlight once again.

THE THEATRE AT ACE HOTEL
929 S. Broadway, Fashion District // theatre.acehotel.com

Rick Astley marks the release of his album *50* with a concert on October 13, 2016.

Photography by Peter Neill of Be-Hookd Digital

GLOBE THEATRE
740 S. Broadway, Historic Core
globetheatre-la.com

LEFT: Originally opened as a playhouse in 1913, the Globe went through several incarnations including becoming a swap meet location before undergoing a restoration and reopening in 2015.

RIGHT: Performer Mosh in the bimonthly burlesque show *TEASE, if you please!*

Photography by Stephen LaMarche

LOS ANGELES THEATRE
615 S. Broadway, Historic Core
losangelestheatre.com

LEFT: The French-Baroque-inspired interior of the theater features carved plaster ornamentation, mirrors and cove-lit murals.

RIGHT: Theatergoers in the lobby for a Cinespia screening of *Breakfast at Tiffany's* on Valentine's Day, 2015. Cinespia (cinespia.org) presents special screening events throughout the year, with a slate of classic films screened at theaters not regularly open to the public.

Photography by Poul Lange

ORPHEUM THEATRE
842 S. Broadway, Historic Core
laorpheum.com

LEFT: The Orpheum Theatre marquee announces L.A. Conservancy's Last Remaining Seats showing of *Footlight Parade*, the 1933 film starring James Cagney and Joan Blondell.

RIGHT: A Last Remaining Seats showing of the 1923 silent film *Safety Last!* accompanied by a live performance on the Mighty Wurlitzer organ. The program (laconservancy.org) presents about 10 modern and classic films each summer.

Photography by Barry Schwartz

THE SHOW MUST GO ON

Six blocks, 12 theaters and lots of history on Broadway.
By Lydia Mack // Illustration by Chris Sharp

1 UNITED ARTISTS THEATRE
Opened in 1927 // 2,214 seats

LITTLE KNOWN FACT: Charlie Chaplin, Douglas Fairbanks, Gloria Swanson and D. W. Griffith built this theatre for their company, United Artists, which they formed to gain independence from the big studios of the time.
THE LATEST: Now known as The Theatre at Ace Hotel, the venue hosts a variety of concerts and events such as Spiritualized, Elvis Costello, *Star Wars* Marathon and L.A. Dance Project.

2 ORPHEUM THEATRE
Opened in 1926 // 2,000 seats

YOU'VE SEEN IT IN: Broadcasts of *American Idol, America's Got Talent,* the seventh and eighth season finales of *RuPaul's Drag Race.*
THE LATEST: The theater's $4 million makeover in 2003 has really paid off. The Orpheum is alive and thriving as a concert venue, film location and movie theater.

3 RIALTO THEATRE
Opened in 1917 // 800 seats

LITTLE KNOWN FACT: The Rialto opened with *The Garden of Allah* starring Broadway favorite Helen Ware.
THE LATEST: Urban Outfitters restored the theater's marquee and opened a retail outlet in December 2013.

4 TOWER THEATRE
Opened in 1927 // 900 seats

LITTLE KNOWN FACT: This theater was the first in Los Angeles to be wired for talking pictures.
THE LATEST: Rumors say it'll be a future home of an Apple store, the first in DTLA.

5 GLOBE THEATRE
Opened in 1913 // 782 capacity

YOU'VE SEEN IT IN: J.Lo's video "On the Floor" (2011) was filmed here.
THE LATEST: Reopened in July 2015. Billed as the spot for parties complete with bottle service and acrobats. Twice a month, the theater hosts *TEASE, if you please!,* a modern burlesque show.

6 LOEW'S STATE THEATRE
Opened in 1921 // 2,450 seats

LITTLE KNOWN FACT: A six-year-old Judy Garland debuted here as Francis Gumm, appearing as part of performance trio The Gumm Sisters in 1929.
THE LATEST: Currently called the State Theatre and home to a Spanish-language church, the Catedral de la Fe.

7 PALACE THEATRE
Opened in 1911 // 1,956 seats originally; 1,068 seats currently

YOU'VE SEEN IT IN: *Dreamgirls* (2006), *The Big Lebowski* (1988) as Maude's apartment and in Michael Jackson's "Thriller" music video (1983).
THE LATEST: After years as a filming location, a $1 million renovation in 2011 opened the theater's doors to concerts, movie screenings and other events.

8 LOS ANGELES THEATRE
Opened in 1931 // 2,000 seats

LITTLE KNOWN FACT: Charlie Chaplin invested his own money to finish this lavish theater in time for the premiere of his movie *City Lights.* With a construction price tag of $1.5 million, it was the most expensive theater built up to that time on a per-seat basis.
THE LATEST: The theater is now earning its money as a film location and event space.

9 ARCADE THEATRE
Opened in 1910 // 1,400 seats originally; 850 seats currently

YOU'VE SEEN IT IN: If you made the unfortunate mistake of seeing *Daredevil* (2003) starring Ben Affleck and Jennifer Garner, you saw the theater's rooftop, with L.A.'s Broadway played off as New York City.
THE LATEST: Retail space in the lobby.

10 CAMEO THEATRE
Opened in 1910 // 900 seats

LITTLE KNOWN FACT: Until it closed in 1991, the Cameo Theatre was the longest continuously operating movie theater in the United States.
THE LATEST: Retail space in the lobby.

11 ROXIE THEATRE
Opened in 1932 // 1,600 seats

LITTLE KNOWN FACT: It was the very last historic theater built on Broadway, designed by famed architect John M. Cooper. Its claim to fame as the only Art Deco theater in the district makes it easy to spot.
THE LATEST: Retail space in the lobby.

12 MILLION DOLLAR THEATRE
Opened in 1918 // 2,024 seats

LITTLE KNOWN FACT: In the 1940s, the theater hosted jazz and big band stars such as Billie Holiday, Artie Shaw and Lionel Hampton.
THE LATEST: Located next door to a thriving Grand Central Market, it's enjoying new life as prime real estate for live events and movie screenings.

DRINKS WITH A VIEW

Settle in for sunset and watch the lights come up in L.A. from one of these rooftop spots.

By Shelley Levitt

When the sun starts going down, head up to one of Downtown's rooftop bars, where the views are as intoxicating as the crafted cocktails. The magic hour is especially magical from the vantage point of a penthouse patio, a sky-high pool deck or an aerial urban lounge. Linger for late-night eats—anything from burgers to bánh mì—and you'll discover the secret that birds have long known: The panoramic vista of Bunker Hill, Pershing Square and the neighborhood's Art Deco towers is well worth some extra flight time before returning to the nest.

THE ROOFTOP AT THE STANDARD
550 S. Flower St., Financial District // 213-892-8080 // standardhotels.com

You can nibble on pretzels, wieners, strudel and beer from the Biergarten. Or settle into a waterbed pod with your favorite book or sweetie. Either way, the views are spectacular. A DJ spins every night.

71Above

Perch

MORE ROOFTOP BARS

71ABOVE
633 W. 5th St., Financial District
213-712-2683 // 71above.com

Nearly 1,000 feet above street level, on the 71st floor of the U.S. Bank Tower, is the highest restaurant west of the Mississippi. To keep the tab down-to-earth, opt for a savory tart and a classic cocktail at the Sky Lounge.

PERCH
448 S. Hill St., Historic Core
213-802-1770 // perchla.com

There is no better way to approach midnight than seated beside a fire pit on the 16th-floor rooftop lounge of this French bistro. Stellar sip: the signature Spicy Concombre—a mix of gin, St. Germain, cucumber, lime and jalapeño.

UPSTAIRS AT ACE HOTEL
929 S. Broadway, Fashion District
213-623-3233 // acehotel.com

This isn't the most verdant rooftop in L.A. The website accurately touts the bar as "bunker-like." But it might be the hippest. Bring a crowd and enjoy a punchbowl of potent cocktails like the blended scotch/apple brandy/ginger/lemon/black tea Capture the Flag.

ELEVATE LOUNGE
811 Wilshire Blvd., Financial District
213-326-9600 // elevatelounge.com

This 21st-floor spot is, as its name suggests, one of L.A.'s most elevated party spots. It's lofty in other ways, too, with sleek décor, bottle service, a very well-dressed crowd and a stunning open-air dance floor.

INTERCONTINENTAL LOS ANGELES SKY DECK ROUND BAR
900 Wilshire Blvd., Financial District
213-688-7777 // ihg.com

Slated to open in the spring of 2017, this spot is perched atop the tallest building west of Chicago, with true bird's-eye views.

WESTIN BONAVENTURE BONAVISTA LOUNGE
404 S. Figueroa St., Financial District
213-624-1000 // thebonaventure.com

The revolving bar on the 34th floor of an iconic L.A. hotel makes a 360-degree rotation in just under an hour. It's the most efficient and *Mad Men*-chic way there is to see the city from every possible perspective.

FIGAT7TH DOWNTOWN LA

at the intersection of LIFE + STYLE

@figat7th · figat7th.com
735 S. Figueroa Street · Downtown L.A.
Across from 7th Street/Metro Center Station
$5 Parking Mon-Fri after 4pm, All Day Sat & Sun

The towering redwood in the four-level atrium has a fireplace at the base and secret passageways through which aerialists move for performances.

DEEP ROOTS

The "cafeteria" where you'll find a giant redwood tree, a tiki bar, a waterfall and a speakeasy all under one roof.

By Bekah Wright // Photography by Poul Lange

A taxidermic bison estimated to be 70 to 90 years old is one of the many mammal exhibits that also include a coyote and a deer.

Stroll past 648 South Broadway on a Friday or Saturday night and the line snaking outside alerts right away: This is no run-of-the-mill cafeteria. True, Clifton's is Los Angeles' oldest surviving cafeteria, but this institution, which was born in 1935 and reclaimed its iconic status in 2015, houses much more than cuisine. Indeed, this "Cabinet of Curiosities" recently changed its moniker to Clifton's Republic.

Step inside the five-level space, and seven restaurant/bar/entertainment venues await, each with treasures to be revealed. The most obvious: a towering artificial redwood tree. One might be inclined to follow the redwood skyward, but enticing aromas delay such a proposition. This establishment, after all, began as an eatery. When Clifton's first opened its doors during the Great Depression, the cafeteria's altruistic side shone forth with this motto: *Pay What You Wish. Dine Free Unless Delighted.* Though this precedent is no longer intact, sentimental menu favorites—like turkey pot pie and short rib chili—are, along with modern-day allures, like Stumptown coffee and artisanal pizza.

The next decision: Go up or down? Choose the latter, and a hidden passageway delivers adventurers to Shadowbox, a veritable archaeological dig located in Clifton's basement. There are artifacts to be discovered, such as a bevy of dinosaur eggs buried at the foot of the bar. Learning their secret might best be undertaken while sipping an experiential libation. Sustenance comes by way of fare from executive chef Andrew Pastore, the head of Clifton's culinary program. There's spontaneous entertainment, too. Cabaret, anyone?

Clifton's second floor pays tribute to California's wild and woodsy side with aptly named cocktails from Monarch Bar (happy hour note—the 1935 price tag for a second round holds fast at 35 cents) that can be imbibed around the sequoia tree trunk's crackling fireplace. Adding ambience is a tiny chapel tucked into a parapet, and a vast population of taxidermic critters, including a bison, no less. Within a glass case resides a bit of romance—a teapot and letter relaying the story behind the vessel's abduction in 1942 by a nostalgic, honeymooning couple.

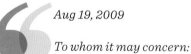

Aug 19, 2009

To whom it may concern:

In Sept 1942 my husband and I were dining at Clifton's cafeteria. We were on our honeymoon! I had admired this silver teapot and unbeknownst to me, as we were leaving, he put his sailor hat on it and took it! It has been in our teapot collection for 67 years and always brought back fond memories! My husband has been gone for 2 years, is he forgiven?

Fondly, Virginia"

The lush décor in the tiki bar, Pacific Seas, includes artifacts and rare pieces from the original Clifton's Pacific Seas.

On Friday and Saturday nights, strains of swing can be heard from the third floor's Brookdale Ballroom and Gothic Bar, where dancers roll out their best Lindy Hop moves to a live band. A hidden staircase winds its way up a level to the fourth floor's Pacific Seas Bar and Art Deco Map Room. A Polynesian vibe, replete with thatched roofs, landscape murals, tiki-style cocktails and mahogany Chris-Craft boat, transports visitors from L.A.'s urban sprawl to tropical islands.

Beyond this paradise is another escape: Treetops Bar. A plethora of empty birdcages charge the memory to flit within their confines. It's not unlikely to spy an aerialist act underway, dangling just outside.

Word is Clifton's is where creative geniuses Walt Disney and Ray Bradbury (look for his restored booth on the third floor) came to fuel up on inspiration. Guests today definitely acquire fodder for their own imaginations. After all, Clifton's is a place where magic lives, with a new wonder beheld with each and every visit.

CLIFTON'S REPUBLIC

648 S. Broadway, Historic Core // 213-627-1673 // cliftonsla.com

DRINK WITH A LION

L.A. local Julia Voth at the lion exhibit, one of the taxidermy dioramas that are a collaboration with the Natural History Museum and include information on how to protect lions, coyotes and bears.

STYLE SQUAD

Pocket Square Clothing has given menswear a bold punch of expression and DTLA trendsetters show how to make it personal.

By Kathy Nenneker // Photography by Allen Daniel

There's a fashionable orbit around the L.A.-based menswear accessories company founded in 2011 by Andrew Cheung and Rodolpho Ramirez. Their philosophy on style, that dressing out of the box is the new normal, has attracted a diverse following to Pocket Square Clothing that includes corporate CEOs, directors, artists, musicians and athletes, all looking to personalize the traditional menswear uniform. "Accessories are the one place where men can really experiment with their wardrobes," Ramirez says about the locally made line that includes ties, socks, lapel pins, tie bars and pocket squares, all pieces that "offer a way for men to express their own personal style." The partners met in college, where Cheung majored in business and Ramirez in architecture, and both are the sons of first-generation immigrants. "Our moms were seamstresses; we learned to sew from them. In the beginning, we were making every single piece in our line," Ramirez says of their start. After operating a series of pop-up shops throughout L.A. in 2016, they opened their Downtown flagship, where they also offer custom suiting available in more than 1,000 fabrics alongside furniture designed by Ramirez. About their home base, Ramirez says, "We're influenced by the culture and identity of Downtown, which is so mixed. We're very much informed by the community around us."

POCKET SQUARE CLOTHING

205 W. 7th St., Historic Core // pocketsquareclothing.com

"The most important finishing touch for me has to be sunglasses. I'm not ready to go or do anything if I don't have some shades on."

—Briggs

> *"I like to add one extra piece. Something to take my outfit to the next level."*
>
> —Parker York Smith

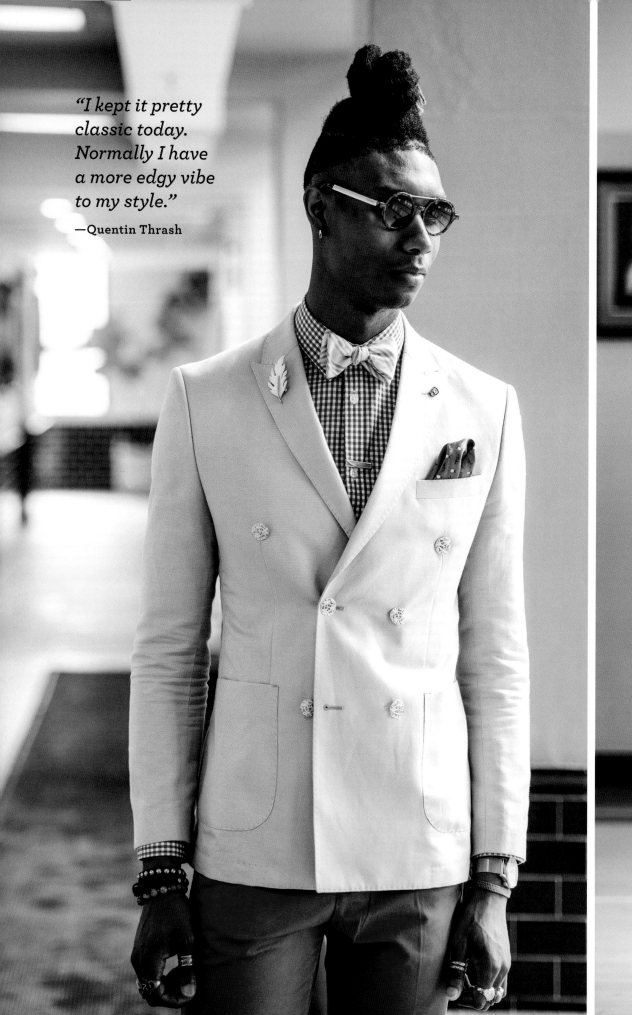

"I kept it pretty classic today. Normally I have a more edgy vibe to my style."

—Quentin Thrash

"My personal style is classic menswear, but I like to experiment with streetwear elements, mixing the two."

—Rome Castille

"I've been wanting to wear these blue suede shoes for some time now, and this was the perfect time to break them out. I went with a more toned-down suit with a little pop of color on the accessory side."

—Briggs

"My personal style is a direct indication of my current mood. It's a unique blend of casual, dapper and trendy. I like to call it Grown Man Casual."

—Smith

"My look for the day was informed by West Coast flavors and colors. I went with a multicolored shirt, yellow elbow patches and sneakers to keep my look more casual."

—Rodolfo Ramirez

Olympiad Los Angeles 1984

"I took on a more regal yet classic look using darker tones and contrasting rich textures to complement the historic interiors of the Los Angeles Athletic Club."

—Andrew Cheung

"My most important finishing touch would be my gold teeth. They keep me rooted to my Southern upbringing."

—Thrash

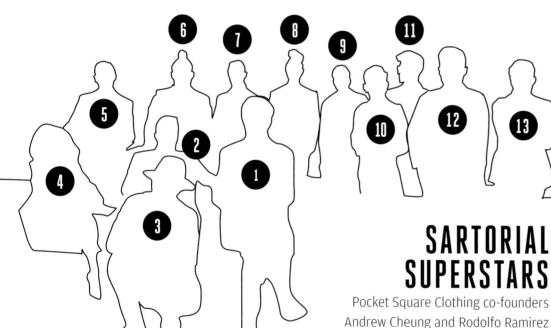

SARTORIAL SUPERSTARS

Pocket Square Clothing co-founders Andrew Cheung and Rodolfo Ramirez and crew photographed on location at the Los Angeles Athletic Club.

431 W. 7th St., Historic Core // laac.com

1. BRIGGS
Creative Director/
Menswear Influencer
briggsbox.com
@briggs
Style Motto: "Wear your clothes, don't let your clothes wear you."

2. JAWN TORRES
Photographer
@jawntorres
Style Motto: "You may not be the best looking, but always look your best."

3. FRANCIS KENNETH
Musician/Blogger
franciskenneth.com
@franciskenneth
Style Motto: "Style is reflected in the way you live, not so much the way you dress."

4. SONIQUE SATURDAY
CEO, Sonique Saturday
soniquesaturday.com
@soniquesaturday
Style Motto: "Don't follow trends; let them follow you."

5. GREG T. BROWN
Model/Influencer
@gregtbrown
Style Motto: "It's not what you wear, it's how you wear it."

6. JASON E.C. WRIGHT
Director, The Vanishing Gallerie;
Director of Operations + Retail,
PSC Flagship
@jasonecwright
Style Motto: "All things in moderation, including moderation. Fit is king."

7. JOHAN KHALILIAN
Writer/Actor/Filmmaker
@johanneus, @laligastyle
Style Motto: "Clothes are an extension of who you are, not who you are."

8. QUENTIN THRASH
Celebrity Barber/Style Influencer
stayflythrash.com
@stayflythrash
Style Motto: "There is no such thing as being overdressed or overeducated."

9. ROME CASTILLE
Record Artist
@romecastille
Style Motto: "Every day is a day to inspire."

10. J. FIG
Menswear Influencer
theruleofthumbs.com
@rule_of_thumbs
Style Motto: "Every guy has a stylish man within him—he just has to be willing to take risks."

11. PARKER YORK SMITH
Journalist
thelooksmith.com
@parkeryorksmith
Style Motto: "Fashion is about looking good; style is about being inspirational."

12. RODOLFO RAMIREZ
Co-Founder/Creative Director,
Pocket Square Clothing
@rodolfo_psc
Style Motto: "Effortless cool."

13. ANDREW CHEUNG
Co-Founder/CEO,
Pocket Square Clothing
@andrewchg
Style Motto: "Fit comes first, everything else is second."

"*My personal style has been described as an elegant time traveler or a tailored mystic.*"

—Jason E.C. Wright

FAST FISH

The James Beard Award-winning chef of the seminal L.A. restaurant Campanile finds a new passion in high-quality seafood dishes served up in minutes.

By Shelley Levitt // Photography by Gabor Ekecs

Paella in a saffron and lobster broth

Many of the people queuing up at Prawn (formerly known as Bombo), the fast-casual fish stall in the center of Grand Central Market, probably don't know that the 60-ish chef working the massive stainless steel cookers is one of the most influential figures in California's culinary history. Mark Peel was the head chef when Wolfgang Puck opened Spago in 1982, and by the end of the '80s he would co-found La Brea Bakery, now a worldwide company, and Campanile, one of L.A.'s top fine-dining restaurants for nearly a quarter century. After Campanile closed in 2012, "I knew I was ready for something new," Peel says, but he had little interest in introducing another white-tablecloth restaurant to L.A.'s food scene. Instead, he says, "I wanted to take what I knew and bend it into something that more people could afford and access."

It was Peel's wife, Daphne Brogdon, host of *Daphne Dishes* on the Food Network, who suggested that his niche might be offering quality fish and seafood at a reasonable price. Peel remembered the steel-jacketed steam kettles that he had seen years ago at Grand Central Oyster Bar in New York City's Grand Central Station. "I loved those," he says. "They're fast, clean, efficient and fun to watch. It's kind of a show." With the hulking kettles installed at Prawn, Peel can deliver broth-based dishes like fish stew, shrimp boil or steamed fish in less than five minutes and for under $15. (Fried chicken, braised short ribs, salads and sandwich rolls are also on the menu.)

Being part of the 100-year-old Grand Central Market with its vibrant mix of new and old vendors is invigorating, Peel says. "There's a great energy and eclecticism here. It gets you out of your bubble and right into the middle of a great cross section of humanity."

PRAWN AT GRAND CENTRAL MARKET

317 S. Broadway, Historic Core // 213-624-2378 // chefmarkpeel.com

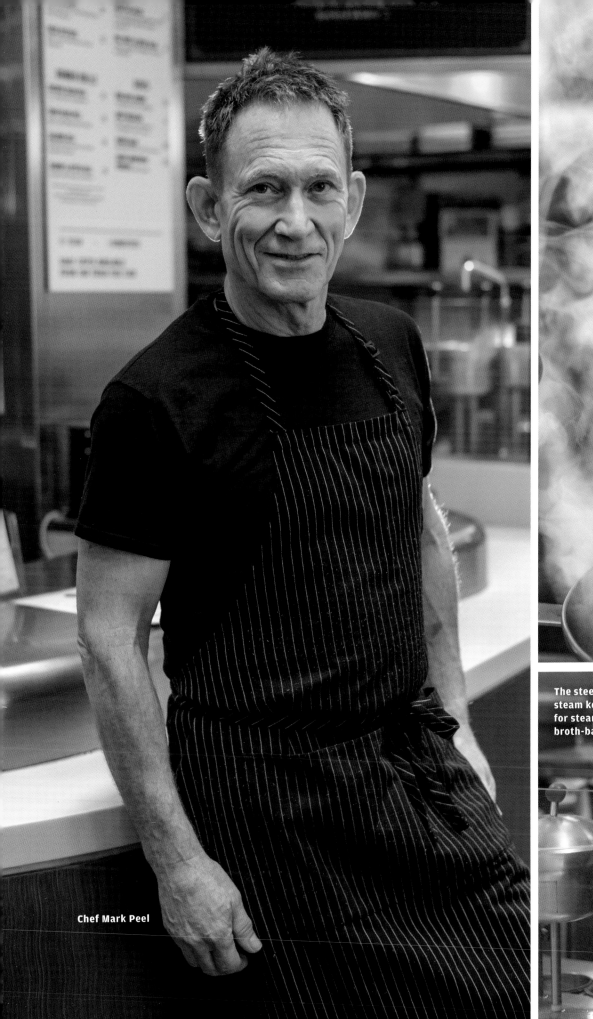

Chef Mark Peel

The steel-jacketed steam kettles used for steaming Peel's broth-based dishes

Installation view of Isa Genzken's
Schauspieler (Actors) (at left) and
Untitled with window, windowsill,
radiator, plants, coins, aluminum
cans and found objects, 2016.

ART CENTER

Hauser Wirth & Schimmel takes aim at the idea of a traditional gallery, creating a context for art in a massive space that includes a bookstore, an education lab, a public garden and a restaurant.

By Shelley Levitt

I f you have an hour or even 30 minutes to spare, you could dart into Hauser Wirth & Schimmel, the new art space that occupies an entire city block in the Downtown Arts District, and breeze through its current exhibit. But you could also pass a very happy day and evening here. The latest, and sixth, outpost of the international gallery Hauser & Wirth, the sprawling arts complex was created to explore a new model "for what an art gallery can be and do," says Iwan Wirth, co-founder and co-president. Opened in March 2016, it fills the restored Globe Mills, a massive collection of interconnected late 19th- and early 20th-century buildings and outdoor space that served as a flour mill. Along with the exhibition galleries, which are devoted to contemporary and modern masters, there's ARTBOOK, a 2,000-square-foot arts and culture bookstore, which offers the full catalog of Hauser & Wirth Publishers as well as rotating retail collections that explore a theme or movement of contemporary and 20th-century art. Bibliophiles will also want to visit the Book & Printed Matter Lab, a separate project that celebrates the vibrant

The first L.A. solo exhibition for the acclaimed late Austrian artist Maria Lassnig, *A Painting Survey, 1950–2007,* in 2016.

A 2016 installation in the gallery courtyard of Isa Genzken's *Rose III,* a 26-foot-tall sculpture modeled after an actual flower Genzken chose and sent to the foundry.

role of books and prints in the life of artists, and regularly hosts talks and panels along with its installations.

The spot on which Hauser Wirth & Schimmel sits was once filled with grapefruit and orange groves, and you might still catch a lingering scent of citrus in the dramatic sculpture courtyard that's designed as a place for the community to gather for urban picnics, conversation or contemplation. Or maybe it's the scent of parsley, rosemary, cilantro or thyme that's catching your attention. The courtyard's kitchen garden supplies all the herbs for Manuela, the on-site restaurant that celebrates the culinary arts with artisanal techniques like in-house smoking, fermenting, preserving and picking. The menu features locally sourced, seasonal ingredients, none more local than the fresh eggs from the dozen rare-breed chickens who make their home in the garden's chicken coop, designed by landscape architects Mia Lehrer + Associates. It's also in the garden where the weekly drop-in tours convene every Thursday at 6:30 p.m. (no RSVP needed). You'll want to check the website for news of other events, which have included everything from artist talks to "Sundays with the Gardener," morning nature walks and workshops on making "wild" beer.

HAUSER WIRTH & SCHIMMEL

901 E. 3rd St., Arts District // 213-943-1620 // hauserwirthschimmel.com

THE GALLERY SCENE

THE BOX GALLERY
805 Traction Ave., Arts District // 213-625-1747 // theboxla.com

Located in the Arts District, The BOX Gallery showcases innovative contemporary art and exhibitions of modern artists. Recent shows have included Barbara T. Smith and Naotaka Hiro.

GRICE BENCH
915 Mateo St.Ste. 210, Arts District // 213-488-1805 // gricebench.com

Owned by artist Jon Pylypchuk and James Bae, this gallery's recent exhibits have included the work of Christina Forrer and Max Jansons.

NIGHT GALLERY
2276 E. 16th St., Butte Street Junction // 323-589-1135 // nightgallery.ca

Davida Nemeroff's gallery has been based in Downtown since 2013 and has become an institution in the L.A. contemporary art scene. The gallery's roster includes artists Mira Dancy and Samara Golden.

ROYALE PROJECTS
432 S. Alameda St., Arts District // 213-595-5182 // royaleprojects.com

Located in a former toy warehouse, Paige Moss and Rick Royale's 6,500-square-foot gallery specializes in the work of emerging and mid-career artists whose work is rooted in either abstract or conceptual art. Royale Project's artists include Phillip K. Smith III, Ken Lum and Alejandro Diaz.

THINK TANK GALLERY
939 Maple Ave., Ste. 200, Fashion District // thinktank.gallery

Located on the second floor of a fabric storage warehouse in the Fashion District, Think Tank Gallery's signature has become its site-responsive exhibits, including the immersive "Break Bread," a 7,000-square-foot cake maze and candied urban block party by artists Scott Hove and Baker's Son.

WILDING CRAN GALLERY
939 S. Santa Fe Ave., Arts District // 213-553-9190 // wildingcran.com

Husband-and-wife dealers Naomi deLuce Wilding and Anthony Cran opened their eponymous gallery in the Lower Arts District in 2014, and like in so many areas of Downtown, the scene has transformed around it, a sure sign being the new Soho Warehouse across the street slated to open in 2018. Recent exhibitions have included the work of Martin Bennett and Karon Davis.

VISION QUEST

Best known for his large-scale black-and-white paintings, artist-photographer-director Tommii Lim is DTLA's answer to the modern Renaissance man, doing it all with bold simplicity.

By Elizabeth Turner

Lim at work in 2015 on a large mural, *Astronaut*, in Atascadero, California.

For artist-photographer-director Tommii Lim, DTLA is the nexus of simple living and creative inspiration. The L.A. native took up residence on Spring Street in 2008, before it became the hub of Downtown nightlife. "I loved it right away," says Lim. "It was a little bit more raw then. I met all different sorts of people—a lot of them are my friends to this day."

As Downtown flourished, so did Lim's creative output. But it all came to a standstill in 2010, when an accident threatened the loss of his right eye. The injury required a year of painstaking recovery before doctors could do a corneal transplant. Then, with a newly installed cadaver's cornea and 24 stitches in his eyeball, Lim faced another full year of recovery, persistent double vision and depression.

"For two years I couldn't make any artwork. It was a big ordeal," he says. "But it was good for me to step back and take a break. I started appreciating my friends, my family. It sounds cheesy, but it just made me appreciate the world."

One of the people who buoyed Lim through his recovery was his manager, the late Karl Bornstein, a charter founder of MOCA. Bornstein immersed his client in Bauhaus, Russian constructivist and '60s minimalist abstract art. "He could see what I liked, and he tried to educate me on the history of it," says Lim. "It really helped me see why I do some of the things that I do."

When Lim picked up the paintbrush again, his work reflected a new goal for art and life: Keep it simple. He focused on expressing everyday interactions and the small moments of life. "It's hard to make something very simple just using the bare essentials. What I do with my paintings is exactly that. And black and white is as basic as you can get."

These days, he's about to do several murals in Downtown Los Angeles. His work adorns the walls of Culver City's upscale Korean BBQ spot Hanjip, which will soon add a Downtown location. As a die-hard Lakers fan, he got a major thrill from a 2016 collaboration with Nike and *Be-Street*

magazine that involved a hand-painted basketball and a video appearance with Kobe Bryant to commemorate Bryant's NBA retirement.

DTLA turned out to be an easy place to simplify a life. Lim ditched his car. He moved to the quieter Fashion District, near his art studio. There he's added photography and video to his bag of tricks. "Painting is cool because I get to do whatever I want," he says. "But it's solitary work. That's why I love video and photography—I get to go out and meet people. What's a creative person without interactions and inspiration?"

BOLD MINIMALIST

ABOVE: The artist in his studio. Cover showcasing Lim's collaboration with *Be-Street* magazine and Nike.

LEFT: Lim's signature sneaker Sona, a project as guest creative director for ASIF.

DÉJÀ VU

A flashback to some of the iconic street corners and historic moments that are reflected in the current resurgence of DTLA.

By Poul Lange

Bustling sidewalks jammed with pedestrians, clanging streetcars and schools of bicycles crowding the asphalt. Twenty-four-hour businesses and scores of restaurants and theaters packed with well-dressed Angelenos. A municipal rail system bigger than that of New York City. It might sound like a Los Angeles city planner's fantasy, but it was a reality in L.A. in the 1920s and '30s, when Downtown was the booming heart of the metropolis.

With over 1,100 miles of rail connecting Downtown with the surrounding counties, and thousands of jobs in the banks and financial institutions along South Spring Street and in the stores of the Jewelry District, the area was in constant movement. A burgeoning entertainment center showcased the celluloid dreams created a couple of miles north in Hollywood. Grand hotels shot up, and Bunker Hill thrived as a wealthy residential neighborhood, full of elegant Victorian mansions. The funicular, Angels Flight Railway, had been in place since 1901, ferrying passengers up Bunker Hill, and in 1939, Union Station opened, effectively connecting Downtown with the rest of the country.

Of course, cars were part of the picture, too. Lots of them. And the automobile eventually came to play an important role in the demise of Downtown. With the development of the Los Angeles freeway system after World War II, residents and corporations moved to the suburbs

In 1946, moviegoers had a choice between the western *The Outlaw*, featuring Jane Russell, and the romantic comedy *Tomorrow Is Forever* with Orson Welles and Claudette Colbert. Today, the Rialto's Art Deco neon marquee heralds the store inside, Urban Outfitters.

The Yellow Cars of the Los Angeles Railway were on track in Downtown. The urban rail system opened in 1901, and at its peak of operation it ran 20 streetcar lines and 1,250 trolleys. In 1945, the railway was sold to National City Lines, a company backed by Firestone Tire, Standard Oil of California and General Motors, among others. Predictably, the trolleys were soon replaced by diesel buses, and the last electric rail car was dismantled in 1963. Coming full circle, in 2016 the L.A. City Council approved the first steps to re-establish a streetcar route in Downtown.

Herald-Examiner Collection/
Los Angeles Public Library

and investments Downtown decreased. Historic buildings were demolished to make room for parking lots that became more profitable than the structures they replaced. The electric trolley system was slowly being dismantled, and the last rail line was shut down in 1963. The Bunker Hill Redevelopment Project (1955) not only razed a thriving residential neighborhood, permanently filled in the Hill Street Rail Tunnel and closed Angels Flight, but also created so much new office space that many of Downtown's remaining commercial tenants moved out of the Historic Core, leaving the district mostly devoid of tenants above ground floor. Suburbanization left its mark in abandoned buildings and empty streets, and Downtown went through a bleak period of deterioration.

Over the past decade, however, a strong movement has been reversing these trends. Political and commercial forces have joined to revitalize Downtown, and the development of L.A. LIVE and the surrounding area fueled a renewal of investment. Residential tenants and creative offices are moving into the newly renovated buildings. Imaginative stores, restaurants and bars are opening at every turn. The Metro system is expanding and connecting Downtown to the rest of the city, and world-class museums and concert halls attract locals and visitors alike.

To celebrate the city's past and the resurgence of the present, this portfolio takes a look back at the streets of L.A.

Although pedestrians normally crowded Downtown streets, May 2, 1910, was not a typical day on the corner of Spring Street and 6th Street. The All Night and Day Bank (a 24/7 operation) had been closed the night before by order of the California Superintendent of Banks. Inside the bank, its president, Newton J. Skinner, sat with a revolver on his desk, guarding the building to keep out "the undesirable element." He told the *Los Angeles Herald*, "There is not the slightest danger of anyone losing any money they have deposited here. Total deposits on hand are $946,000. I have locked it in the safe." Outside the bank, depositors lined up in an attempt to withdraw their funds.

USC Libraries, California Historical Society Collection, 1860–1960

THEATRE
LOEW'S STATE
SPRECKELS BLDG.
BROCKMAN BUILDING
NEW YORK STORE
SHOE CO
Mandel's
LOEWS STATE
NORMA SHEARER
CONRAD NAGEL
"WANING SEX"
RUBE WOLF
FANCHON-MARCO
NORMA SHEARER IN THE WANING SEX
WITH CONRAD NAGEL
CONRAD NAGEL
THE OWL DRUG CO
STOP

LEFT: Women dressed in the popular "flapper" style that characterized the modernist era of the Jazz Age cross 7th Street by Broadway in 1926. For a contemporary take on the same view, see page 7.

RIGHT: The invention of the "safety bicycle" in the late 1880s instigated one of the biggest bicycle booms of all time. A police squad at Broadway and 5th Street takes advantage of the technical advances, riding alongside horseless carriages and the newly installed tracks of the streetcar system.

Security Pacific National Bank Collection/Los Angeles Public Library

MOVERS & SHAKERS

A roundtable with five Downtown denizens who are finding creative ways to preserve the best of DTLA's community spirit.

By Elizabeth Turner // Photography by Joshua Spencer

They came Downtown for a variety of personal and business opportunities, but they stayed for the refreshingly tight-knit community. On a sunny December morning in 2016, a group of young entrepreneurs gathered at the Reserve Vault City Club (RVCC), a private social club situated on the ground floor of the historic Federal Reserve Bank building. There they chatted about the neighborhood's collaborative spirit and their creative efforts to help their neighbors on Skid Row successfully transition out of homelessness.

ON DISCOVERING DTLA SPIRIT

Brad Robinson: I came from the East Coast, where I'm used to neighborhoods—I knew my neighbors, and I had an interest in their lives. When I came to L.A., it was just sprawl. I lived in Hollywood, the Hollywood Hills, Eagle Rock, all around. I never knew my neighbors. But when I moved Downtown 10 years ago, everyone in the building came and introduced themselves.

Juan Pablo Torre: For me it's a similar feeling. And the reason why this happened is that I was looking into being

in an environment where I feel better—like in Europe, in Madrid, where we all know each other and there's a community. You know people by name, you say, "Hey, how are you?" And if something happens, if you need help in some way, it's "Hey Chris, I need this. Do you know anyone?" That is the feeling I started to have here.

Robinson: We live in a culture that gives a lot of attention to self, but Downtown, it's about engaging with other people.

Chris Cota: I agree with that. We all share in each other's successes and do events with each other, but we share in

Chris Adams, founder of Reserve Vault City Club (RVCC), a members-only social club supporting the culture of Los Angeles. RVCC occupies the ground floor of DTLA's Federal Reserve Bank building, a Classical Moderne gem built in 1929.

Brad Robinson, corporate relations and events manager for Skid Row Housing Trust, an organization that provides permanent supportive housing to more than 1,800 individuals who have experienced homelessness, prolonged extreme poverty, disabilities, mental illness and/or addiction. In 2016, Robinson developed the Skid Row Denim Academy as a fashion-forward way to benefit the cause.

Juan Pablo Torre, classically trained chef and managing director of Tuck Ventures, a hospitality group, has developed and managed boutique hotels in Europe and the United States and is currently focused on the U.S. His latest project, The Tuck Hotel, opened in 2016 on Spring Street.

Chris Adams

Brad Robinson

each other's failures, too. If any of us is coming up short or in need in any way, we're quick to lean on each other. That doesn't happen anywhere else that I've experienced.

Torre: I found this property on Spring Street—or actually it found me—and I said, "Look, we can do a hotel here." I was thinking I'd be here one year, and it became four years. At one moment I thought: I could sell or I could keep going. I decided to keep going because I started to feel comfortable with all the good things happening here—the community embrace, being accepted as a Latin immigrant, it's really important. RVCC has a lot of Asians and Mexicans and Latins from all over. It's this mixed community that makes Downtown a beautiful spot.

Chris Adams: My phone rings a lot with people who are looking for help in navigating Downtown, in getting an

understanding of the culture and of the community.

Cota: I met Chris Adams when I was moving Skingraft headquarters from one side of Downtown to the other. He helped us find our new space. Brad started helping us out a couple years ago. It started with parties, but it's become much more than that.

Adams: RVCC was started to create this sanctuary, a spot that represents what we all fell in love with about Downtown in the first place. And then also to show new people who come into town what our culture is like Downtown—to share with the old and the new, to set that platform, that understanding of what we're trying to do down here. You join with the understanding that you're not here to forcefully connect with people, because we have so many false connections these days. Only when you shed

Juan Pablo Torre

Chris Cota

Brit Moore Gilmore

those layers of false connection can you truly, authentically connect with somebody.

Robinson: When I moved here, I wasn't looking for anything other than the fact that I could get a 1,500-square-foot loft for $1,200 a month. I also understood why that loft was at that price. It was Skid Row–adjacent. I had no problem living in an urban environment—I actually prefer it. People who live on the streets of Skid Row are part of our community as well, so I was getting to know them. I interacted with them.

ON FASHIONING NEW SOLUTIONS

Brit Moore Gilmore: Originally [The Giving Keys founder] Caitlin Crosby saw this couple, Rob and Cera, on the sidewalk in Hollywood. They were holding a sign that said "ugly, broke and hungry." She felt compelled to meet them, take them out to dinner and hear their story. During dinner she complimented Cera's necklace. Cera's response was "Thank you, I actually make jewelry. I made this." Caitlin realized, "Oh my gosh, I'm doing this thing called The Giving Keys…I should hire you guys to do this." Literally she proposed the idea to them at that dinner. The next day she took them to Pep Boys and got all the engraving equipment, and they started making keys for her.

Robinson: Skid Row Housing Trust was working with the Avery Dennison company, which had moved to the Arts District. In 2015 they held a Denim Summit where they brought in all the major denim houses for which they make labels. That's where I learned how much of the denim manufacturing materials come from Los Angeles.

Chris Cota, CEO and co-owner with his brother, designer Jonny Cota, of the DTLA-based fashion house Skingraft. Founded in 2006, Skingraft specializes in leather-centric luxury streetwear worn by celebrity clients including Rihanna and Beyoncé.

Brit Moore Gilmore, president of The Giving Keys, a jewelry company and bridge employer for people transitioning out of homelessness. At the company's Arts District workshop, employees stamp inspiring words onto repurposed keys to makes necklaces and other jewelry.

RAW POWER

Messaging inside Skid Row Denim Academy's The Advocate jacket ($300, skidrowdenimacademy.org) reminds the wearer of its philanthropic purpose.

I said, "What if we made denim with our messaging on it to make people look differently at how to participate in the solution?"

So I pitched this crazy idea, and within six months we had a line. For a $300 donation, you can get a pair of high-end selvedge denim pants or a jacket. And every time someone puts it on, they see this messaging. If someone says, "Juan Pablo, that's a great jacket," you can say, "Let me tell you why I'm a great person for wearing it."

So we've created a way for people to talk about it. Chris Cota was very helpful with our first launch event on the rooftop of The Standard hotel. We were able to move $20,000 worth of denim.

Cota: It was a phenomenal night. Everyone really came together. It was great.

Robinson: The denim is very cool, but Skid Row Housing Trust is really the thing. It's an amazing company with over 26 buildings, over 1,800 formerly homeless people housed. We work with the top architects. Our buildings are LEED-certified platinum. Our motto is housing first. Before we can deal with the many reasons people suffer from long-term homelessness, we think, "Let's see what happens when you have a roof over your head, a door that locks."

Cota: Brad hit it on the nose. We've been down here for 10 years. Downtown is awesome, and it's become cooler every year. But the underbelly of it doesn't go away. We're a family company and we've always wanted a way to tap into the community. Brad just came along with the path of least resistance to do that.

Gilmore: Housing is the most important step initially to get people stabilized. But then giving them purpose and income through a job is really important. And I would say the purpose piece is almost more critical—having somewhere to be, something to do, people who are counting on you. The Giving Keys is committed to creating as many jobs as we possibly can for people who are transitioning out of homelessness. We've created more than 60 job opportunities since we started. Our headquarters is in the Arts District. We give tours a lot because we want to give people the opportunity to see it all in action and meet our team. It's a really inspiring environment because it's a such a diverse group, with people from all different walks of life coming to the same place to work. I think there's a lot that happens by osmosis in that environment, too.

Robinson: Homelessness is a huge problem. But when you look at it as just a problem, you can talk yourself out of any kind of participation, saying, "What can I possibly do?" Just showing up is the most important thing. You start seeing there are real solutions working right now, every day, that are changing lives.

Gilmore: A really important realization for me was how close I could be to being in that situation. There are so many reasons why people experience homelessness. Sometimes it can feel like us and them. But how many Americans do you know who are living paycheck to paycheck? What if they were to experience some sort of medical crisis or the death of a spouse? Or people you might know who struggle with more socially acceptable forms of addiction: What if it went a bit further and they were overcome by it? We're just not that far from being in that position, but we think we are.

PAY IT FORWARD
The concept of The Giving Keys (thegivingkeys.com) is to wear a word you need, embrace that message and then pass on your key to someone who needs it more than you do.

DESIGN DUO

Husband-and-wife team Scott Jarrell and Kristan Cunningham live, work and curate in the Arts District.

By Shelley Levitt // Photography by Maiko Naito

Whether they're considering acquiring a piece for Hammer & Spear, their design showroom and studio in the Downtown Arts District, or for their tri-level loft that's just a few blocks away, husband-and-wife designers Scott Jarrell and Kristan Cunningham ask themselves the same question: Is it the very best version of that item? From a $7,500 platform sofa by Neri & Hu for De La Espada to a $7.50 brass pencil, "we don't bring anything into our home or our store unless we both truly love it," Cunningham says.

Their aesthetic, which Cunningham describes as "masculine and attainable," has attracted a fervent following. It began with their friends. "People would walk into our home and say, 'I want to live here,'" Cunningham says. (The couple has lived in 11 different homes in Los Angeles since moving here from Boone County, West Virginia, two decades ago.) When they opened Hammer & Spear in March 2013, the store quickly became a design destination and they've since redoubled their space to 5,000 square feet.

Around a third of that space is devoted to their interior architecture business. Together with their team, they've worked on projects that range from designing the homes

Scott Jarrell and Kristan Cunningham at home with their dog, Bean.

Located in the Barker Block Lofts, the couple's residence showcases their signature look, a thoughtfully selected mix of vintage finds and pieces created by local artisans.

RIGHT: Hanging behind a velvet chair is a 1960s-era American Automobile Association map of Southern California that Jarrell found in the garage at an estate sale.

BELOW: A piece by California artist Judith Foosaner.

The kitchen and dining areas provide a workshop for a mix of textures and materials.

A vintage find on display

of TOMS founder Blake Myscokie in Topanga Canyon and Jackson Hole, Wyoming, to creating the interiors for a sprawling commercial-residential Arts District project.

Cunningham is a DIY diva and the former host of HGTV's *Design on a Dime,* so it's no surprise that their home is filled with vintage finds, rescued from flea markets, Craigslist, auctions and estate sales. "We're collectors," Cunningham says. "Or, as we like to say, 'fancy hoarders.' We love beautiful handmade things. The store is a way for us to support our collecting habit."

The furniture, housewares and lifestyle goods at Hammer & Spear are largely curated from contemporary artists and artisans, many of whom reside in the Arts District. "Living and working in an area that's so dense with talent makes for a very nice way to run a business," Jarrell says. Some of the couple's favorite Downtown fabricators include (wh)ORE HAüS welder/furniture designer Meyghan Hill, fabric artist Mary Little, lamp designer Christopher Kreiling and ceramicist Jonn Coolidge. As informal ambassadors of the Downtown arts scene, "our goal has always been to provide a platform for as many artists as we can," Cunningham says. "We feel a responsibility to get their work out there and to say to the larger design community, 'Hey, look at what the Arts District has to offer!'"

UNDER-GROUND ART

Creating a sense of place and reflecting history, the architecture, murals and designs of L.A.'s Metro system make getting around just part of the experience.

By Bekah Wright // Photography by Mark Esguerra

Los Angeles is an expansive city, to say the least. Getting around the metropolis via the L.A. Metro system brings with it many benefits, among them opportunities to be immersed in art. What Metro commuters realize right away is that this isn't some humdrum subway—it's the heartbeat of Los Angeles.

When plans for the Metro began back in the 1970s, actor George Takei, who served on the Southern California Rapid Transit District's board of directors, was adamant about integrating art into the transit experience. The fruition of his efforts can be seen throughout the Metro's meticulous design, where neighborhood stations represent a sense of place. Indeed, step into the Hollywood/Vine station and artist Gilbert "Magu" Luján's film reels and "yellow brick road" bring on nostalgia for Hollywood's film industry. Stars of another kind can be seen at the Vermont/Sunset station, where artist Michael Davis combined medical symbols and celestial orbits, tips of the hat to nearby hospitals and Griffith Park Observatory.

Not only can travelers take in permanent art installations, but there are temporary exhibitions as well. A current one to catch is the *Through the Eyes of Artists...* poster series

At the famous intersection of Hollywood and Vine, the station design incorporates symbols of the history and glamour of the film industry, including two original film projectors from the 1930s donated by Paramount Pictures.

displayed both on Metro trains and buses. Local artisans conceived many of the posters, another step in keeping with the Metro's desire to imbue a feeling of community. "We believe art creates a heightened sense of place, engages riders, encourages the use of public transit and improves the quality of life throughout L.A. County," says Heidi Zeller, creative services manager for the L.A. County Metropolitan Transit Authority.

These works have caught the attention of the public, resulting in more than 10,000 annual participants in Metro's art tours, activities and events. Even performing arts take place, with music, dance, poetry readings and film readings hosted at Union Station.

In keeping with the scrupulously designed metro system, artwork is integrated into stations while complying with technical, safety and durability requirements. These same considerations were made when designing The Bloc station, which opened in December 2016. Referred to as an "anti-mall," this mixed-use space includes hotel accommodations, dining and retail shops.

The Bloc's 7th Street Corridor location is a snap for Metro passengers to access through a new pedestrian tunnel linked to the 7th Street/Metro Center station. "The tunnel will bring that station up to four entrance/exit/access points," says Metro Communications Manager Rick Jager. "It both integrates into the urban fabric of the area and increases visibility to potential system users."

As goals go, Metro's design could be considered an ongoing mission accomplished, bringing functionality and community together as one.

More than 2,000 film reels line the vaulted ceiling of the Hollywood/Vine station.

"The California Dream" is the theme of the North Hollywood station, where nearly 4,000 square feet of hand-painted tile murals recognize the diversity and aspirations of generations of immigrants to the area.

DOWNTOWN AREA METRO STATIONS

Metro makes it easy to get to attractions including the Hollywood Bowl, Chinatown, Universal Studios and the Santa Monica Pier.

Gold Line continues to Highland Park, Pasadena and Azusa ↑

CHINATOWN

UNION STATION

LITTLE TOKYO STATION

To East L.A. →

Temple St.

Grand Park

1st St.

CIVIC CENTER STATION

2nd St.

The Broad

MOCA

3rd St.

Grand Central Market

4th St.

PERSHING SQUARE STATION

7TH STREET TRANSFER STATION

Metro Lines in DTLA

Red Line
North Hollywood to Union Station

Purple Line
Wilshire/Western to Union Station

Blue Line
Downtown L.A. to Long Beach

Expo Line
Downtown L.A. to Santa Monica

Gold Line
East Los Angeles to Azusa

5th St.

Los Angeles Central Library

Pershing Square

6th St.

← Red Line continues to Hollywood and Universal City

7th St.

← Purple Line continues to Wilshire/Western

Figueroa St.

Flower St.

The Bloc

Hope St.

Grand Ave.

Olive St.

Hill St.

Broadway

Spring St.

Main St.

Los Angeles St.

Blue Line continues to Watts Towers, Compton and Long Beach ↓   ↓ Expo Line continues to USC/Exposition Park, Culver City and Santa Monica

TIME MACHINE

Three historic venues offer a flashback to a storied past.

By Katherine Sullivan

Cranes dot the Downtown skyline and DTLA buzzes with shiny new luxury developments, but thoughtful redevelopment and creative caretakers have nurtured back to life some of the city's most illustrious properties. Stepping into these clubs, restaurants and theaters is like traveling back in time to L.A.'s heady years of speakeasies and underground bars. Also in the mix are locations that successfully mash up then and now, nightclubs that flash with lasers and pulse with EDM in carefully preserved cultural landmarks.

In the Art Deco Oviatt building, well-dressed couples at the Cicada Club relive the swing era, dancing to live music in one of Downtown's most elegant spaces, while blocks away, one of DTLA's hottest nightclubs, Exchange LA, pulses in the former home of the Pacific Coast Stock Exchange. In the Higgins Building basement, the city's first power plant has been transformed into The Edison, an Art Deco–inspired nightclub lounge with retro cocktails and live music.

CICADA RESTAURANT AND CLUB

617 S. Olive St., Financial District // cicadarestaurant.com

On specially scheduled nights the Cicada Club swings with 1920s- and '30s-style live music and dancing. Cameron McCormick takes in the view of the dance floor from the mezzanine.

Photography by Marko Prelic

LITTLE-BIG BAND

LEFT: Phat Cat Swinger performs live at Cicada, August 2016.

RIGHT: Dancers on the floor during the performance of Phat Cat Swinger.

Photography by Marko Prelic

EXCHANGE LA
618 S. Spring St., Historic Core
exchangela.com

DJ Jackal at on stage during a
performance, August 2016.

Photography by Allen Daniel

THE EDISON

108 W. 2nd St., Historic Core
edisondowntown.com

LEFT: A performance of Big Willie's Burlesque featuring live jazz during cocktail hour.

RIGHT: At the main bar, mixologists serve up signature cocktails, including The Edison with Woodford Reserve barrel bourbon, pear cognac, lemon and honey.

Photography by Alexander Laurent

A PAGE OUT OF TIME

Housed in a century-old bank building on Spring Street is a surprising enterprise that has defied the odds.

By Matt Villano // Photography by Poul Lange

There are two reasons why owner Josh Spencer chose the name "The Last Bookstore" for his iconic bookshop in Downtown L.A. First, it was a bit of a joke: A bunch of bookstores were closing when the place opened in 2009, and the idea was this would be the last bookseller to open, ever. Perhaps more dramatically, Spencer hoped to convey that his bookstore would be the last one customers would ever need to patronize, since the place carries everything they could possibly want.

Whichever explanation you prefer, The Last Bookstore is the place in DTLA to celebrate the printed word. The store stocks 250,000 titles at any given time—new books, used books, coffee-table art books and more. It sponsors readings. It throws signings. It hosts a weekly open-mic night. There are even original sculptures made of real books, including a tunnel through which you can walk.

Spencer is more than just the owner of this beloved shop; he's the lifeblood. The 41-year-old dad became a paraplegic after a horrific moped accident in 1996, and has overcome his disability with panache. He's the man behind the sculptures, the guy who books the talent, the one with the vision to convert a 101-year-old bank building on Spring Street into a place for the local book-loving community to eschew their tablets and smartphones and come together to flip pages of the paper variety.

"Books have never stopped being something people revere and enjoy," says Kate Orphan, the store manager. "As long as people still love them, we'll be here."

THE LAST BOOKSTORE

453 S. Spring St., Historic Core // 213-488-0599 // lastbookstorela.com

For more on Josh Spencer, watch *Welcome to the Last Bookstore,* an award-winning documentary by director Chad Howitt. vimeo.com/139828664

The Last Bookstore houses over 250,000 titles in 22,000 square feet of space.

The Labyrinth Above the Last Bookstore.

A towering sculpture of books by David Lovejoy.

SIGHTS BY BIKE

Bookended by two of the city's architectural icons, City Hall and The Music Center, Grand Park has bike-friendly entrances and ramps throughout the 12-acre space. Access the park along the bike lane on Spring Street and be sure to visit the splash pad adjacent to the Arthur J. Will Memorial Fountain.

Model: Emi Rose Kitawaki; hair & makeup by Laura Dee Shelley; outfit by Lanston Sport

STREET CYCLE

Want to get from STAPLES Center to Grand Central Market or from Chinatown to MOCA? Metro Bike Share makes it easy with more than 65 bike stations throughout DTLA.

Photography by Ian Spanier

L os Angeles is gaining speed as a multimodal city, particularly when it comes to two-wheeled transport. Indeed, when Bicycling.com put out its 2016 list of the 50 Best Bike Cities in the U.S., L.A. was ranked 24th, a notable improvement from its previous position as 28th. There are many reasons why L.A. is becoming more bike-friendly, among them accessibility to bike share programs. DTLA's Metro Bike Share (bikeshare.metro.net) program is making it easier than ever to grab a set of wheels and explore Downtown.

HOW IT WORKS

GET A BIKE from any Metro Bike Share station, go for a ride and then give it back at any station.

FIND A DOCKING AREA with Metro's online bike map (bikeshare.metro.net/stations) or app (bikeshare.metro.net/app).

PAY AT THE STATION KIOSK with a debit or credit card. The rate is $3.50 for the first half hour and $3.50 for each half hour after that.

RIDE ANY TIME OF THE DAY. Bikes are available 24/7/365.

CALL OR TEXT 844-857-BIKE for customer service.

BIKE SANTA MONICA

Breeze Bike Share is a 500-bike system sponsored by Hulu that services Santa Monica and Venice with more than 80 rental hubs (the bikes and docks of Metro Bike Share and Breeze are not interchangeable). Traversing the area's 100 miles of bike lanes is also economical with a pay-as-you-go plan costing $7 per hour. Other conveniences come via the smart bikes' built-in GPS systems and U-lock. Download the app at santamonicabikeshare.com/#app.

CYCLE SAFETY

BEFORE YOUR RIDE

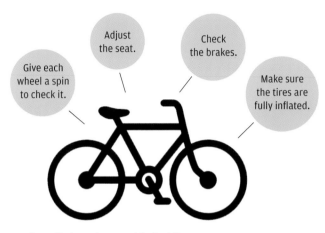

Give each wheel a spin to check it.

Adjust the seat.

Check the brakes.

Make sure the tires are fully inflated.

If you find any issues with the bike, contact customer service and select a different bike.

DURING YOUR RIDE

✓ You should always wear a helmet. Riders under age 18 are required to wear one by law.

✓ Minimize riding on the sidewalk. Always yield to pedestrians.

✓ Every lane is a bike lane. People on bikes may use a whole lane.

✓ Watch for open car doors and cars turning right.

✓ Always ride in the same direction as traffic.

✓ Avoid the "door zone." Give clearance to parked cars. Trust us, you don't want to be surprised by a car door being opened.

✓ Never ride with headphones; it's important to hear what's going on around you.

✓ Always pass on the left. Use your bell or say "On your left" to let pedestrians and riders know you're passing.

For more safety recommendations, visit bikeshare.metro.net/how-it-works/riding-tips.

POINTS OF VIEW

A historic icon and a modern tower offer two takes on an epic vista of the city and beyond.

OUE SKYSPACE LA

633 W. 5th St.,
Financial District
oue-skyspace.com

HEIGHT
1,018 FEET

YEAR COMPLETED
U.S. BANK TOWER: 1989
OUE SKYSPACE LA: 2016

ADMISSION
$25 (GENERAL)
$33 (SKYSLIDE COMBO)

OBSERVATION LEVEL
70TH FLOOR

Thrill seekers are rewarded with a sky-high view from the 45-foot-long Skyslide.

Digital features in the entrance area include an "infinity mirror" and a time-lapse view of the city.

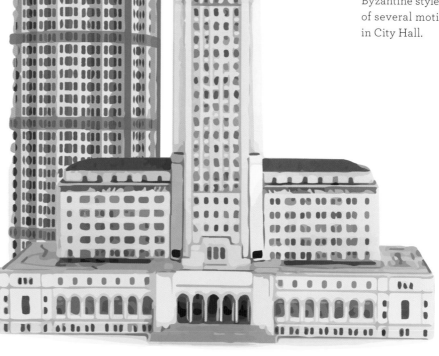

LOS ANGELES CITY HALL

200 N. Spring St.,
Civic Center
lacity.org
Bring your valid ID and enter from the Main Street side.

HEIGHT
454 FEET

YEAR COMPLETED
1928

ADMISSION
FREE

OBSERVATION LEVEL
27TH FLOOR

The observation deck is open on weekdays from 8 a.m. to 5 p.m.

Byzantine style is one of several motifs used in City Hall.

Passion is What Drives You.

It embodies us all. Whether you own a coffee shop, curate an art gallery, teach at a yoga studio or are just a free spirit, passion is what drives you to seek a new twist on an old classic. Much like how Downtown L.A. has been revitalized and reinvigorated, we as humans love finding new ways to explore our passions. Let Subaru help you explore the "new" Los Angeles and reconnect with why you fell in love with this city.

SUBARU.

Confidence in Motion

URBAN HIKE

Sprint through the concrete canyons of DTLA for a good workout and an up-close view of some of the town's most popular architectural landmarks.

Photography by Ian Spanier

For an outdoor training session with great views the stairways, parks and hills of Downtown can easily give Runyon Canyon and Griffith Park a run for their money. This trek will take you through stainless steel canyons designed by architect Frank Gehry, by a lake that sits atop a parking lot and along the entire length of a railway line. While you probably won't meet coyotes or rattlesnakes on your metropolitan trek, you might encounter hummingbirds, parrots and Pomeranians.

WALT DISNEY CONCERT HALL

Most concertgoers head straight into the Frank Gehry-designed home of the Los Angeles Philharmonic, but take the stairway on Grand Avenue near 2nd Street to the rooftop Blue Ribbon Garden for a look at another side of the masterpiece. Pause for a breather to enjoy the year-round blooming landscape and the sculpture *A Rose for Lilly* (see page 94), a fountain designed by Gehry as a tribute to the late Lillian Disney. Then pick the pace back up and run the paths and stairways that wind up the building's stainless steel-clad exterior.

JOHN FERRARO BUILDING
Why does a town in perpetual drought have a building surrounded by a reflecting pool? The 1.2-million-gallon body of water that reflects the home of the Los Angeles Department of Water & Power actually serves a function for the building: The filtered recirculated water operates as part of the HVAC system.

DOROTHY CHANDLER PAVILION,
THE MUSIC CENTER

CALIFORNIA PLAZA

ANGELS FLIGHT

A Rose for Lilly, Blue Ribbon Garden, Walt Disney Concert Hall.
Model: Emi Rose Kitawaki; hair & makeup by Laura Dee Shelley; outfit by Lanston Sport

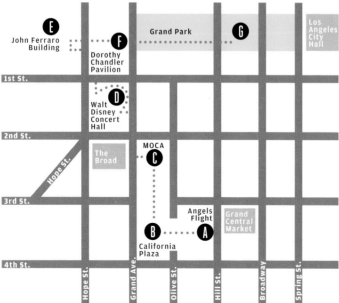

URBAN HIKE ROUTE

A ### ANGELS FLIGHT
351 Hill St., Bunker Hill // angelsflight.org
This historic funicular opened in 1901 to transport prominent citizens just 298 feet up and down the slope between Hill and Olive streets. Seen most recently in the film *La La Land,* the railway is not currently running, although efforts continue to get the beloved trains back in service. Start at the base of Angels Flight on Hill Street, take the stairs (153 steps) to up to Bunker Hill and enter California Plaza.

B ### CALIFORNIA PLAZA
350 S. Grand Ave., Bunker Hill // grandperformances.org
Atop Bunker Hill sits this open-air plaza in the shadow of two towers. Featuring a water court and amphitheater, the plaza is host to "Grand Performances," a popular free concert series each summer. Cross through the plaza to the Omni Hotel Los Angeles, then take the pedestrian walkway to the plaza at MOCA.

C ### THE MUSEUM OF CONTEMPORARY ART (MOCA)
250 S. Grand Ave., Bunker Hill // moca.org
Located in the plaza outside the museum, one of Nancy Rubins' largest sculptures has an equally outstretched name: *Chas' Stainless Steel, Mark Thompson's Airplane Parts, About 1,000 Pounds of Stainless Steel Wire and Gagosian's Beverly Hills Space.* Cross Grand Avenue to Walt Disney Concert Hall.

D ### WALT DISNEY CONCERT HALL
111 S. Grand Ave., Bunker Hill // laphil.com
The fourth venue of The Music Center complex, the hall is acclaimed for its architecture and acoustics and has become one of L.A.'s most recognizable architectural landmarks. Exit the Blue Ribbon Garden to 1st Street, then cross Hope Street to the John Ferraro Building.

E ### JOHN FERRARO BUILDING
111 N. Hope St., Civic Center
Bunker Hill's first high-rise, this architectural icon has been a popular film location since its opening in the mid-'60s. The structure and reflecting pool were featured in the dream sequences of *Inception,* where CGI effects added buildings to the pool and height to the building. Cross Hope Street back to the Music Center.

F ### DOROTHY CHANDLER PAVILION
135 N. Grand Ave., Civic Center // musiccenter.org
The grande dame of The Music Center complex, the Dorothy Chandler is home to the LA Opera and Glorya Kaufman Presents Dance at The Music Center. Cross North Grand Avenue to Grand Park.

G ### GRAND PARK
200 N. Grand Ave., Civic Center // grandparkla.org
Flanked by The Music Center and City Hall, this 12-acre park dotted with fountains, pink benches and lawns hosts rotating food trucks Tuesday through Thursday each week.

DISTANCE: Approximately 1.3 miles

Looking for some
drama tonight?

CENTER THEATRE GROUP | DTLA

Ahmanson Theatre
Big, bold, and Broadway.

Mark Taper Forum
**Explosive, provocative
theatrical experiences.**

See what's up at
CTGLA.org

Located on the Music Center Plaza | **213.628.2772**

Phillipa Soo and Adam Chanler-Berat. Photo by Joan Marcus.

Fiesta Fabric

Flower District

Miyazaki's dog, Danger, sits in as a sounding board.

The designer meets with her pattern maker, Takako Storey.

FASHION DISTRICT

The area bordered by Central Avenue and Santee Street is the working heart of the clothing industry in L.A. Designer Natashia Miyazaki navigates its alleys, wholesale stores and markets with ease.

Photography by Alexander Laurent

The bustling streets of this compact district—with small textile shops crammed from floor to ceiling, vast flower markets, warehouses and discount vendors—are frequented by professionals, bargain hunters, students and stylists. It can all be a bit intimidating to the casual visitor, but Natashia Miyazaki finds inspiration here along with resources. "There is a lot of stuff to sift through, but it makes it so much more rewarding when you find a deal or an amazing piece of fabric."

8:00 A.M. SHOPPING FOR PROPS at THE FLOWER DISTRICT

242 and 766 Wall St., Fashion District // laflowerdistrict.com

The wholesale warehouses of the Los Angeles Flower Market and the surrounding flower malls cover several city blocks and house an astounding selection of blooms. Though the trade gets first pick, most shops open to the public at 8 a.m. Monday, Wednesday and Friday, and 6 a.m. Tuesday, Thursday and Saturday. Miyazaki gravitates to lilies, peonies and tropical flowers for photo shoots, and arrives early for the freshest cuts.

Blossom

Chicken Pho at Blossom

ABOUT

Natashia Miyazaki lived in London, designed for Guess in Hong Kong and moved to L.A. for love. After a stint at iconic L.A. brand Nasty Gal, she became her own Girlboss and now funnels her passion into Paper Machine, her line of ready-to-wear that's made entirely in DTLA. "This is my epicenter. I've got everything I need within walking distance."

10:00 A.M. COLLABORATING at WORK

Miyazaki works in one of the many '20s-era high-rises that have been converted to live/work lofts. "DTLA reminds me more of European cities. I love the architecture."

1:30 P.M. WORKING LUNCH at BLOSSOM

426 S. Main St., Fashion District // blossomrestaurant.com

The reward for finding this small Vietnamese café is some of the best pho and spring rolls in Downtown. "I love being surrounded by life and culture, and living in metropolitan areas with high populations. It keeps me inspired when lots of cultures come together in one melting pot," Miyazaki says.

3:00 P.M. SOURCING at FIESTA FABRIC and X TRIMS & LEATHERS

1142 E. 12th St., Fashion District // fiestafabric.com
811 Maple Ave., Fashion District // xtrimsandleathers.com

"I am surrounded by inspirations—trims, leather, beads, gems, lace, sequins. It's a feast for my creative soul," says Miyazaki of the many resources in the area. Two of her favorites include Fiesta Fabric for luxe laces and velvets and X Trims & Leathers for hardware trims and studded chokers.

5:00 P.M. NETWORKING BREAK at COFFEE COLAB

305 E. 8th St., Ste. 103, Fashion District // coffeecolab.com

Miyazaki's enterprising spirit carries over to the café she co-owns with her husband, William Miyazaki, and others. Their secret weapon is an iced espresso with condensed and whole milk (code-named Bruce Lee). "I have met so many people through this place. Ironically, it has nothing to do with fashion, but because it's a cool hangout in the center of the Fashion District, it's a gold mine!"

6:30 P.M. CREATIVE MEETING on THE ROOFTOP DECK

Miyazaki has one last meeting with a drink and view. "It is a really interesting time to be living in DTLA. Lots of new people are moving into Downtown and starting to cultivate a really cool vibe of creatives and entrepreneurs."

Rooftop meeting with Daniya Mussina, Creatives DTLA

Coffee CoLab

MORE TO EXPLORE FASHION DISTRICT

BY GRACE JIDOUN

EAT
PREUX & PROPER
840 S. Spring St., Fashion District
213-896-0090 // preuxandproper.com

Is it a vivacious bar? A boozy brunch spot? Or an elegant restaurant? Thankfully, this soul food restaurant is all of the above, mixing Creole and Cajun spice with a seasonal Cali sensibility. Grab a seat on the charming balcony and dig into étouffée and beignets.

EAT
L.A. CHAPTER
927 S. Broadway., Fashion District
213-235-9660 // lachapter.com

Located in the historic Ace Hotel, this transporting spot is esteemed for its upscale yet unpretentious New American cooking. The brasserie setting is perfect for a pre-show dinner; the adjacent Theatre at Ace Hotel hosts dance and live entertainment in a restored Spanish Gothic setting.

EAT
1810 RESTAURANT
105 W. 9th St., Fashion District
213-623-1810 // 1810restaurant.com

For no-holds-barred, live-fire cooking, try this cozy Argentine restaurant (named after the Argentina revolution of 1810), specializing in authentic churrasco. Large platters of steaks, short ribs, chicken and fish are complemented by papas fritas and empanadas.

EAT
WOODSPOON
107 W. 9th St., Fashion District
213-629-1765 // woodspoonla.com

Brazilian native Natalia Pereira explores the street food of the Minas Gerais region at this friendly, stylish storefront. The fabulous feijoada black bean stew, yucca fries and chicken pot pie are best devoured with homemade sangria. Don't miss Saturday brunch, where Pereira's baking skills are on display.

EAT
SONORATOWN
208 E. 8th St., Fashion District
213-290-5184 // sonoratownla.com

The taco is the go-to street food in L.A., but this casual, funky storefront is doing something different with it. The northern Mexican-style taco consists of a hand-made flour tortilla filled with delectable mesquite-grilled meats. Also find Chorizo from L.A.'s top purveyor, the Chori-Man. Open Tuesday through Saturday, 11 a.m to 4 p.m.

DRINK
PATTERN BAR
100 W. 9th St., Fashion District
213-627-7774 // patternbar.com

Pattern Bar embraces its location at the epicenter of the Fashion District, serving specialty cocktails named after famous designers and incorporating vintage sewing machines and irons into its elegant, high-ceiling space. The Old World setting gets 21st-century fresh when live DJs pump up the crowd Thursday through Saturday.

SHOP
LAST FRIDAY SAMPLE SALE
9th St. & Los Angeles St., Fashion District

Achieve instant local status by hitting the sample sales on the last Friday of the month, where wholesale showrooms throw open their doors to the public. Ones to check out: California Market Center, Cooper Design Space, Gerry Building and The New Mart, all located at the intersection of 9th and Los Angeles streets.

SHOP
THE SANTEE ALLEY
210 E. Olympic Blvd., Fashion District
213-488-1153 // thesanteealley.com

With more than 150 discount retail stalls packed into this two-block pedestrian-only stretch, it's like an open-air bazaar. From cocktail dresses to workout gear, fancy phone cases and fancy footwear, there's always something to buy that you didn't know you needed.

SHOP
TANNER GOODS
860 S. Broadway, Fashion District
213-265-7480 // tannergoods.com

This Portland-based company is dedicated to the art of leather working, and it pulls out all the stops with premium materials and hand-stitched detailing at its Fashion District location. You'll find sleek bags, belts and wallets alongside selvedge denim.

ARTS DISTRICT

The section of Downtown bordered by Little Tokyo and the Los Angeles River is both home and a source of inspiration to food stylist John Anthony Galang.

Photography by Alexander Laurent

The creative in John Anthony Galang is fully at home in the Arts District, the location of urban artists' studios since the 1970s. The area, like the rest of DTLA, is going through a rebirth, with new galleries, restaurants and shops springing up seemingly overnight.

11:00 A.M. FOOD PROP SHOPPING at URBAN RADISH

661 Imperial St., Arts District // urban-radish.com

For research and sustenance, Galang shops at this market and eatery with its carefully curated selection of gourmet products, farm-fresh foods and organic fruits and vegetables. From the commercial kitchen at the center of the store come nutritious, made-from-scratch dishes for breakfast, lunch and dinner.

12:30 P.M. LUNCH BREAK at RESIDENT

428 S. Hewitt St., Arts District // residentdtla.com

Housed inside a three-story former metal shop and warehouse is this funky, laid-back bar, beer garden and music venue. The outdoor garden area with its picnic tables, string lights and succulents echoes the Austin music scene. "My favorite drink is the New Fashioned with bourbon, sweet potato liqueur, brown sugar and toasted pecan bitters."

Urban Radish

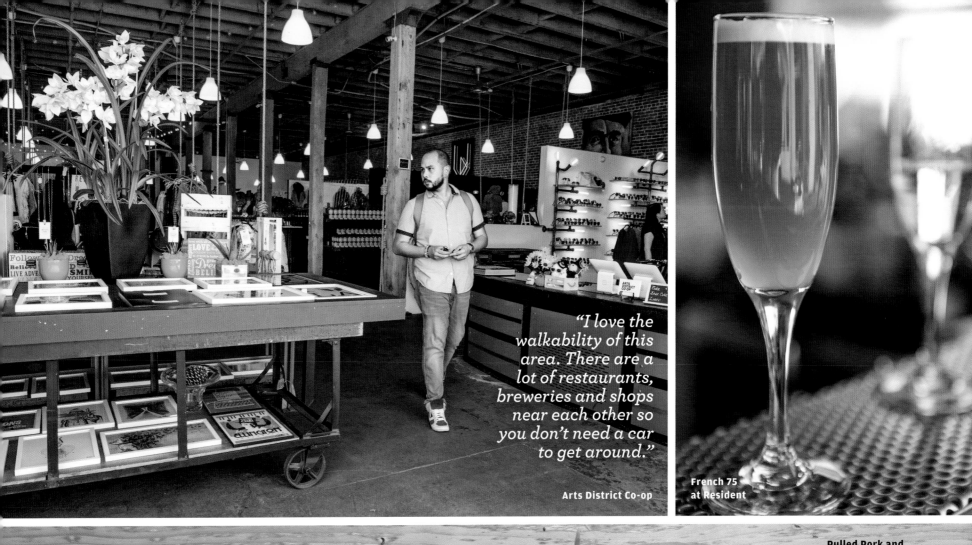

"I love the walkability of this area. There are a lot of restaurants, breweries and shops near each other so you don't need a car to get around."

Arts District Co-op

French 75 at Resident

Pulled Pork and Egg Sandwich, Fried Chicken Salad and New Fashioned at Resident

Apolis: Common Gallery

Salt & Straw

ABOUT
A graduate of the Kitchen Academy (now Le Cordon Bleu College of Culinary Arts), John Anthony Galang worked at a number of Hollywood restaurants before he realized his passion for food styling. He developed his skills working with mentors on the sets of cooking shows and photo shoots. "A lot of hours are spent making the most perfect burger, tacos or pizza."

1:30 P.M. SHOP FOR A CAUSE at APOLIS: COMMON GALLERY

806 E. 3rd St., Arts District // apolisglobal.com

"Classically stylish menswear with a story" can be found at this gallery-like shop founded by brothers Raan and Shea Parton with the philosophy that business can create social change. A globally sourced selection of menswear and accessories, including hand-knit alpaca sweaters from Peru and jute market bags assembled by a collective of mothers in Bangladesh, are displayed alongside rotating artist exhibitions.

2:00 P.M. STUDY DESSERT at SALT & STRAW

829 E. 3rd St., Arts District // saltandstraw.com

"I'm an ice cream nerd and my most favorite flavor combination is the Stumptown Coffee & Compartes Love Nuts and Salted, Malted, Chocolate Chip Cookie Dough on a waffle cone," Galang says. The name's a mouthful, but it will be worth trying at this well-loved shop known for its one-of-a-kind flavors (hello Black Olive Brittle & Goat Cheese).

2:30 P.M. PLAY HARD AND DRINK WELL at EIGHTYTWO

707 E. 4th Pl., Arts District // eightytwo.la

Galang advises a fuel-up at Blue Bottle Coffee, then a stop at this classic arcade with its rotating collection of 50 pinball and arcade machines, full bar and outdoor patio.

3:30 P.M. RESIST SPONTANEOUS BUYS at ARTS DISTRICT CO-OP

453 Colyton St., Arts District // adcoopla.com

For props and unique pieces, Galang frequents this spot with its eclectic mix of vendors selling everything from bikes to vintage pieces and artwork.

4:15 P.M. INSPIRATION SEARCH at ROYALE PROJECTS

432 S. Alameda St., Arts District // royaleprojects.com

In the two airy galleries of this 6,500-square-foot space, Galang seeks a break and inspiration. Recent shows have included the minimal colorful works of David Allan Peters and the mixed-media exhibition "Shine Time."

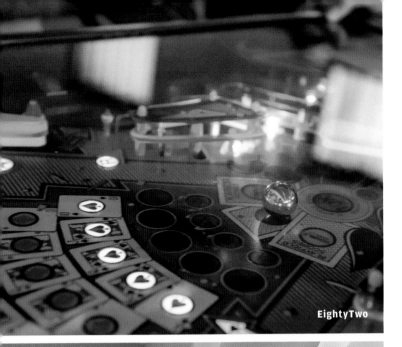
EightyTwo

Royale Projects

MORE TO EXPLORE ARTS DISTRICT

BY GRACE JIDOUN

EAT
VILLAINS TAVERN
1356 Palmetto St., Arts District
213-613-0766 // villainstavern.com
A bevy of craft beers and updated classic cocktails fuel the bohemian spirit at this dark, atmospheric hangout. After kicking back a few, tear into elevated bar snacks and comfort food dishes while enjoying live music on the outdoor stage.

EAT
EAT.DRINK.AMERICANO
923 E. 3rd St., Arts District
213-620-0781 // eatdrinkamericano.com
A creative crowd sips and eats their way through a snacktastic menu of ultra-fresh charcuterie, vegan soups, sandwiches and flatbreads at this locavore gastropub. Exposed brick, rough-hewn wood and vintage couches set the scene for lounging.

EAT
THE FACTORY KITCHEN
1300 Factory Pl., Arts District
213-996-6000 // thefactorykitchen.com
On the ground floor of a converted warehouse, this sophisticated Italian restaurant has "date night" written all over it. The traditional antipasti will entice, but the unfathomably tender pastas are what the Kitchen is known for.

EAT
LITTLE BEAR
1855 Industrial St., Arts District
213-622-8100 // littlebearla.com
Get your *flamande* fix at this bright industrial beer hall that serves Belgian fare like rich beef stew, burgers with truffle aioli, Belgian fries and imported brews. On weekends, the charming spot opens its doors at 10 a.m. for a fabulous brunch that includes waffles, and doesn't close them until midnight.

DRINK
ARTS DISTRICT BREWING COMPANY
828 Traction Ave., Arts District
213-817-5321 // 213hospitality.com
This industrial brewpub continues to offer some of the best artisanal craft beer in the city. But with a Ping-Pong table, darts, vintage Skee-Ball machines and cornhole, you may just want to move in here. When the munchies strike, order pizza from Neal Fraser's Fritzi, which has a take-out window right inside the brewery.

SHOP
HENNESSEY + INGALLS
300 S. Santa Fe Ave., Ste. M, Arts District
213-437-2130 // hennesseyingalls.com
One of the largest booksellers of its kind, the 5,000-square-foot store at One Santa Fe focuses on art, architecture and design (SCI-Arc architecture school is right across the street). Prepare to discover a trove of rare books along with one of the biggest magazine racks in the city.

SHOP
ALCHEMY WORKS
826 E. 3rd St., Arts District
323-487-1497 // alchemyworks.us
This airy boutique feels like a prop-styled paradise for indie designers. Shelves are lined with hand-stitched leather bags, vintage-inspired sunglasses, clothing from local labels and fine textured pottery. For one-of-a-kind gifts, it's not to be missed.

SHOP
POKETO
820 E. 3rd St., Arts District
213-537-0751 // poketo.com
The husband-and-wife team behind Poketo sources stylish yet functional products created by artists from around the world. The adorable shop is filled with quirky stationery, wooden toys, home essentials, leather goods and more.

DO
THE SPRINGS
608 Mateo St., Arts District
213-223-6226 // thespringsla.com
A day of renewal awaits at this chic, relaxing wellness hub. Choose from more than 35 weekly yoga classes, revitalize with a session of chi renewal or acupuncture, then recharge at the juice bar/café with a smoothie or vegan lunch bowl.

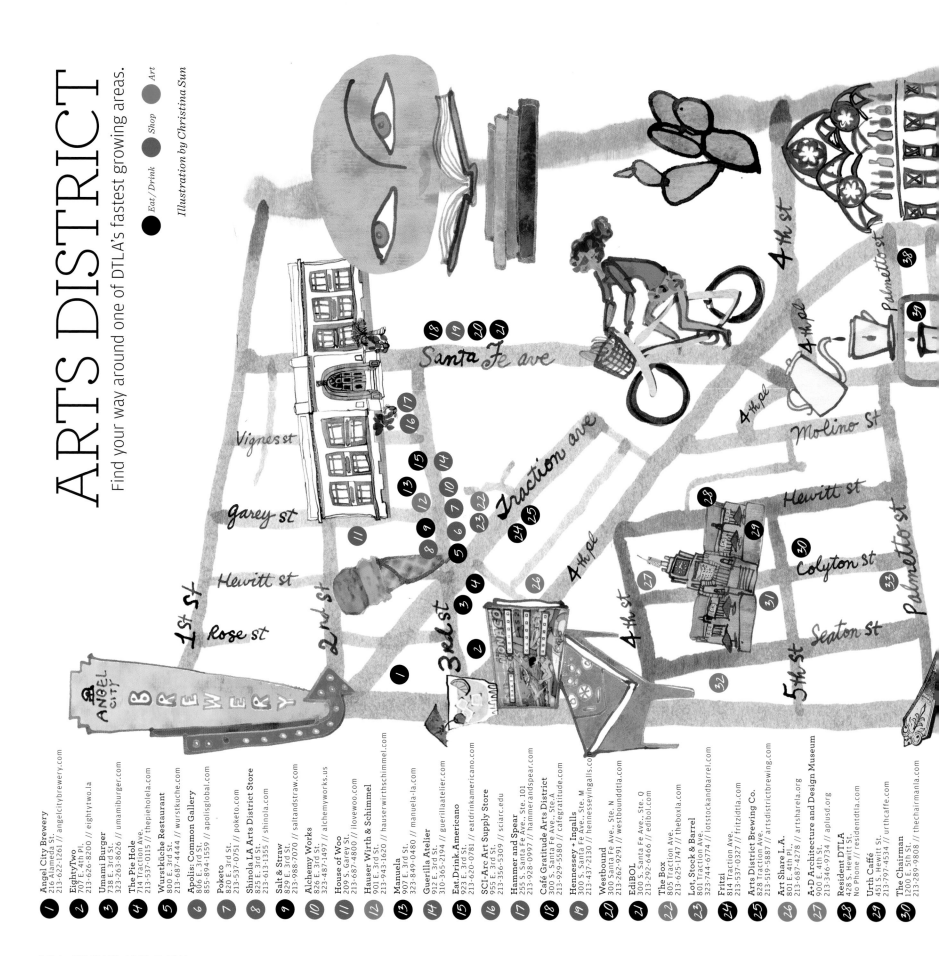

ARTS DISTRICT

Find your way around one of DTLA's fastest growing areas.

● Eat/Drink ● Shop ● Art

Illustration by Christina Sun

1 **Angel City Brewery**
216 Alameda St.
213-622-1261 // angelcitybrewery.com

2 **EightyTwo**
707 E. 4th Pl.
213-626-8200 // eightytwo.la

3 **Umami Burger**
738 E. 3rd St.
323-263-8626 // umamiburger.com

4 **The Pie Hole**
714 Traction Ave.
213-537-0115 // thepieholela.com

5 **Wurstküche Restaurant**
800 E. 3rd St.
213-687-4444 // wurstkuche.com

6 **Apolis: Common Gallery**
806 E. 3rd St.
855-894-1559 // apolisglobal.com

7 **Poketo**
820 E. 3rd St.
213-537-0751 // poketo.com

8 **Shinola LA Arts District Store**
825 E. 3rd St.
213-613-1355 // shinola.com

9 **Salt & Straw**
829 E. 3rd St.
213-988-7070 // saltandstraw.com

10 **Alchemy Works**
826 E. 3rd St.
323-487-1497 // alchemyworks.us

11 **House of Woo**
209 S. Garey St.
213-687-4800 // ilovewoo.com

12 **Hauser Wirth & Schimmel**
901 E. 3rd St.
213-943-1620 // hauserwirthschimmel.com

13 **Manuela**
907 E. 3rd St.
323-849-0480 // manuela-la.com

14 **Guerilla Atelier**
912 E. 3rd St.
310-365-2194 // guerillaatelier.com

15 **Eat.Drink.Americano**
923 E. 3rd St.
213-620-0781 // eatdrinkamericano.com

16 **SCI-Arc Art Supply Store**
955 E. 3rd St.
213-356-5309 // sciarc.edu

17 **Hammer and Spear**
255 S. Santa Fe Ave., Ste. 101
213-928-0997 // hammerandspear.com

18 **Café Gratitude Arts District**
300 S. Santa Fe Ave., Ste.A
213-929-5580 // cafegratitude.com

19 **Hennessey + Ingalls**
300 S. Santa Fe Ave., Ste. M
213-437-2130 // hennesseyingalls.co

20 **Westbound**
300 Santa Fe Ave., Ste. N
213-262-9291 // westbounddtla.com

21 **EdiBOL**
300 S. Santa Fe Ave., Ste. Q
213-292-6466 // edibol.com

22 **The Box**
805 Traction Ave.
213-625-1747 // theboxla.com

23 **Lot, Stock & Barrel**
801 Traction Ave.
323-744-6774 // lotstockandbarrel.com

24 **Fritzi**
814 Traction Ave.
213-537-0327 // fritzidtla.com

25 **Arts District Brewing Co.**
828 Traction Ave.
213-519-5887 // artsdistrictbrewing.com

26 **Art Share L.A.**
801 E. 4th Pl.,
213-687-4278 // artsharela.org

27 **A+D Architecture and Design Museum**
900 E. 4th St.
213-346-9734 // aplusd.org

28 **Resident DTLA**
428 S. Hewitt St.
No Phone // residentdtla.com

29 **Urth Caffé**
451 S. Hewitt St.
213-797-4534 // urthcaffe.com

30 **The Chairman**
1200 E. 5th St.
213-289-9808 // thechairmanla.com

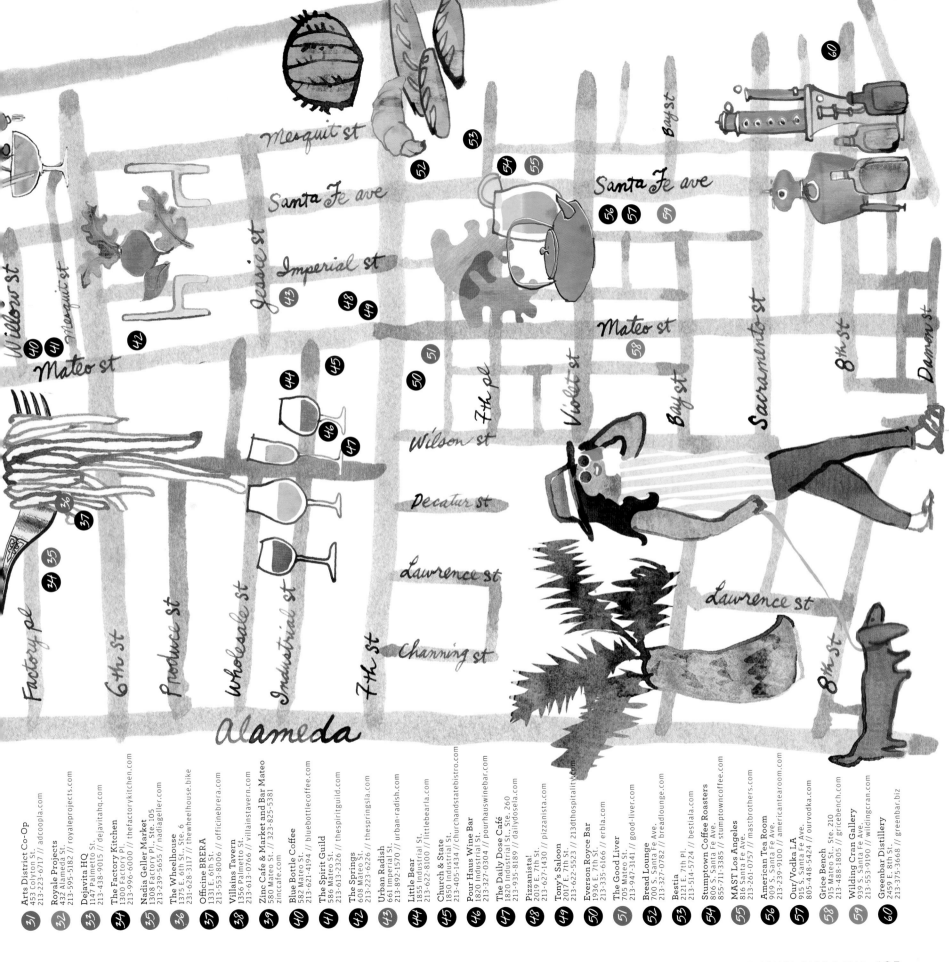

Mesquit st

Santa Fe ave

Santa Fe ave

Bay st

Imperial st

Jessie st

Willow st

Mesquit st

Mateo st

Mateo st

Violet st

Bay st

Sacramento st

8 th st

Damon st

7th pl

Wilson st

Decatur st

Lawrence st

Lawrence st

Channing st

8 th st

Factory pl

6 th st

Produce st

Wholesale st

Industrial st

Mateo st

7 th st

Alameda

31 Arts District Co-Op
453 Colyton St.
213-223-6717 // adcoopla.com

32 Royale Projects
432 Alameda St.
213-595-5182 // royaleprojects.com

33 Dejavita HQ
1147 Palmetto St.
213-438-9015 // dejavitahq.com

34 The Factory Kitchen
1300 Factory Pl.
213-996-6000 // thefactorykitchen.com

35 Nadia Geller Market
1308 Factory Pl., Ste. 105
213-239-5655 // nadiageller.com

36 The Wheelhouse
1375 E. 6th St., Ste. 6
231-628-3117 // thewheelhouse.bike

37 Officine BRERA
1331 E. 6th St.
213-553-8006 // officinebrera.com

38 Villains Tavern
1356 Palmetto St.
213-613-0766 // villainstavern.com

39 Zinc Cafe & Market and Bar Mateo
580 Mateo St. // 323-825-5381
zinccafe.com

40 Blue Bottle Coffee
582 Mateo St.
213-621-4194 // bluebottlecoffee.com

41 The Spirit Guild
586 Mateo St.
213-613-2326 // thespiritguild.com

42 The Springs
608 Mateo St.
213-223-6226 // thespringsla.com

43 Urban Radish
661 Imperial St.
213-892-1570 // urban-radish.com

44 Little Bear
1855 Industrial St.
213-622-8100 // littlebearla.com

45 Church & State
1850 Industrial St.
213-405-1434 // churchandstatebistro.com

46 Pour Haus Wine Bar
1820 Industrial St.
213-327-0304 // pourhauswinebar.com

47 The Daily Dose Café
1820 Industrial St., Ste. 260
213-935-8189 // dailydosela.com

48 Pizzanista!
2019 E. 7th St.
213-627-1430 // pizzanista.com

49 Tony's Saloon
2017 E. 7th St.
213-622-5523 // 213dthospitality.com

50 Everson Royce Bar
1936 E. 7th St.
213-335-6166 // erbla.com

51 The Good Liver
705 Mateo St.
213-947-3141 // good-liver.com

52 Bread Lounge
700 S. Santa Fe Ave.
213-327-0782 // breadlounge.com

53 Bestia
2121 E. 7th Pl.
213-514-5724 // bestiala.com

54 Stumptown Coffee Roasters
806 S. Santa Fe Ave.
855-711-3385 // stumptowncoffee.com

55 MAST Los Angeles
816 Santa Fe Ave.
213-261-0757 // mastbrothers.com

56 American Tea Room
909 S. Santa Fe Ave.
213-239-9100 // americantearoom.com

57 Our/Vodka LA
915 S. Santa Fe Ave.
805-448-5424 // ourvodka.com

58 Grice Bench
915 Mateo St., Ste. 210
213-488-1805 // gricebench.com

59 Wilding Cran Gallery
939 S. Santa Fe Ave.
213-553-9190 // wildingcran.com

60 Greenbar Distillery
2459 E. 8th St.
213-375-3668 // greenbar.biz

Los Feliz Village
Farmers Market

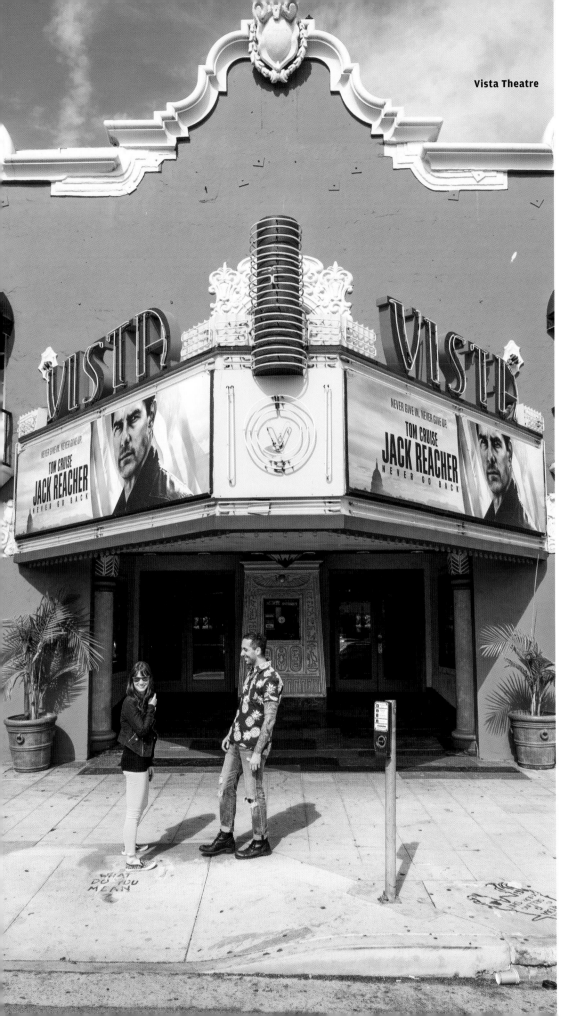

Vista Theatre

LOS FELIZ

When you work at one of L.A.'s most chic concept shops, where do you go to chill out? Charles Worthington III shares his favorite places for California comfort food, a good read and a blast of karaoke.

Photography by Alexander Laurent

C harles Worthington III works at Just One Eye, the luxury retail shop in Hollywood where pieces from Seraphin, Valentino, Gucci and Alexandre Vauthier are displayed alongside artwork by Takashi Murakami and Sterling Ruby, all housed in the Art Deco former headquarters of Howard Hughes' empire. On any given day, celebrity stylists, international tourists and reality stars stop in to pick up the latest must-haves. To get back down to earth, Worthington frequents his neighborhood favorites. "When I get home from work, I can park and walk to restaurants, bars, stores, anywhere."

11:30 A.M. BRUNCH at SQIRL

720 Virgil Ave., East Hollywood // sqirlla.com

At Sqirl, which serves up the height of "new California cooking" with a sunny outdoor patio and a line outside the door, Worthington orders owner/chef Jessica Koslow's signature dish, a sorrel pesto grain bowl with preserved Meyer lemon. The hip café serves global-inspired breakfast and lunch, and its seasonal small-batch jams (try strawberry rose geranium) are where it all started.

1:00 P.M. MEET A FRIEND at LOS FELIZ VILLAGE FARMERS MARKET

Los Feliz Post Office, 1825 N. Vermont, Los Feliz

What this amiable neighborhood market lacks in size,

Sorrel Pesto Grain Bowl at Sqirl

Skylight Books

it makes up for in charm, with local favorites like La Bahn Ranch eggs, Me Gusta Gourmet Tamales and Rocchio Family Coffee Roasters, and some of L.A.'s friendliest vendors.

1:30 P.M. BOOST MENTAL STIMULATION at SKYLIGHT BOOKS

1818 N. Vermont Ave., Los Feliz // skylightbooks.com

Because "reading is good for your brain," Worthington regularly stops in at this shop, frequented by local artists, musicians, writers and scholars. On a typical night you might find a reading-group meeting or a Q&A like the recent one with actor Jon Hamm and writer/reviewer Alan Sepinwall about *TV (The Book)*.

3:00 P.M. ENJOY A FILM at VISTA THEATRE

4473 Sunset Dr., Los Feliz // vintagecinemas.com

Opened originally in 1923 as the Lou Bard Playhouse, the Vista is a mash-up of Spanish and Egyptian decorative styles. Retrofitted with a state-of-the-art sound system, the theater plays first-run films and locals enjoy the plush super comfy seats. The best part? The retro price, $9.50 for general admission, $6.50 for matinees.

5:30 P.M. STOCK UP at CAP N' CORK JUNIOR MARKET

1674 Hillhurst Ave., Los Feliz

This is the place to score that hard-to-find pale ale

Cap n' Cork Junior Market

Blue Goose Lounge

or lager. Cap n' Cork's vast selection of craft beers is constantly rotating, and the wine and spirits selections are impressive, too.

10:30 P.M. SHARE SHOTS at BLUE GOOSE LOUNGE

5201 Sunset Blvd., East Hollywood

Take the side door entrance to this hidden dive bar, where the karaoke rocks, the drinks are stiff and the leather couches are deep.

ABOUT

Charles Worthington III is a fashion stylist, a craft he says "is like being a DJ of the fashion world because you are taking other people's art and making it into something new." Originally from Chicago where he worked at Ikram, Worthington moved to L.A. in 2014. His experience at Prada and Maxfield led him to Just One Eye in Hollywood.

MORE TO EXPLORE EAST HOLLYWOOD / LOS FELIZ / SILVER LAKE

BY GRACE JIDOUN

EAT
TACOS TU MADRE
1824 N. Vermont Ave., Los Feliz
323-522-3651 // tacostumadre.com
From red velvet churros to inventive tacos, fabulous fusion Mexican cuisine has arrived in Los Feliz. This tiny jewel box of a space serves up its own brand of killer Cal-Mex street food amid colorful Día de Los Muertos murals.

WATCH
THE VIRGIL
4519 Santa Monica Blvd., East Hollywood
323-660-4540 // thevirgil.com
Enjoy specialty craft cocktails at this sultry speakeasy-style bar that hosts DJs, dancing and happy hour Monday through Saturday. If you're lucky, you'll catch the Monday night comedy show *Hot Tub with Kurt and Kristen* as you sip espresso-infused rum long into the night.

DRINK
TENANTS OF THE TREES
2808 Hyperion Ave., Silver Lake
323-284-8631 // tenantsofthetrees.com
Enter this unmarked venue and you'll feel like you've landed in someone's magical, candlelit backyard. This indoor-outdoor bar boasts a raucous dance room, but most go to the leafy lounge to chill under the trees with house-infused cocktails.

EAT
CHURRO BOROUGH
1726 N. Vermont Ave., Los Feliz
323-662-0341 // churroborough.com
The churro ice cream sandwich is a cult favorite at this Los Feliz sweets shop, but don't forget to explore the unsung amazingness of the paletas (Mexican ice pops) and imaginative sorbets. Everything here is handmade in small batches daily.

DRINK
ROCKWELL TABLE & STAGE
1714 N. Vermont Ave., Los Feliz
323-669-1550 // rockwell-la.com
Perhaps the most beautiful of all the city's small performance spaces, this Los Feliz supper club is opulently decked out with Baroque chandeliers and a coral tree on the patio. Wednesday nights bring Jeff Goldblum and the Mildred Snitzer Orchestra, giving more reason to linger over the seasonal Cali cuisine.

SHOP
MOLLUSK SURF SHOP
3511 Sunset Blvd., Silver Lake
323-928-2735 // mollusksurfshop.com
Mollusk goes beyond beach threads—though the clothing is high quality and made in California—with a well-curated selection of essential gear. The store is stocked with Liddle custom surfboards, wetsuits, bodyboards, sunglasses and other beachgoer goodies.

EAT
BOO'S PHILLY
4501 Fountain Ave., Silver Lake
323-661-1955 // boosphilly.com
Get a true taste of Philly at this casual mini-chain. With 30 years of experience selling hoagies in New Jersey, the Korean mom-and-pop owners enlisted their grown kids to launch this joint, which combines a hip-hop vibe with meltingly gooey cheesesteaks.

DRINK
GOOD LUCK BAR
1514 Hillhurst Ave., Los Feliz
323-666-3524 // goodluckbarla.com
The kitschy cocktail game is so impressive here, you'll be sipping out of a coconut in no time. Curved red booths, Chinese lanterns and indie bands on the jukebox add up to one charming dive bar. Try the Potent Potion, an aptly named blend of spiced rum, fresh pineapple juice and fresh coconut cream.

SHOP
MOHAWK GENERAL STORE
4011 W. Sunset Blvd., Silver Lake
323-669-1601 // mohawkgeneralstore.com
At this cozy storefront, which sells both women's and men's clothing, Silver Lake's self-employed creatives peruse racks of both indie and designer labels, jewelry and mid-century furniture. Where else can you pick up a Commes de Garçon's top and a vintage turntable all in one swoop?

Cassell's Hamburgers

Bunless burger at
Cassell's Hamburgers

Taejo Kickboxing

Dragon's Breath,
Chocolate Chair

K-TOWN

The best way to experience this diverse and dense part of town is on foot; you'll risk missing the restaurants, cafés and shops tucked behind nearly every storefront if you zip through by car. Media professional Eunice Hwangbo uncovers some of the area's best hidden gems.

Photography by Alexander Laurent

"I love how diverse Koreatown is. Despite the name, there are large Latino, Filipino and Bangladeshi populations as well. Because it's still pretty affordable and central to other areas in Los Angeles, it's also quickly becoming a hip place for creatives and foodies to live, work and play," says Eunice Hwangbo about her neigborhood. Known for karaoke, The Line Hotel and Roy Choi's multiple restaurants, K-Town (as locals call it) also has Art Deco buildings, palm-lined streets and one of the country's best Oaxacan restaurants, Guelaguetza.

12:30 P.M. LUNCH at CASSELL'S HAMBURGERS

3600 W. 6th St., Koreatown // cassellshamburgers.com

"A classic L.A. burger joint, Cassell's recently reopened at the newly revamped Hotel Normandie. I haven't had a chance to try their delicious-looking pies yet, but I can attest to their delicious beef patties that are ground and made in-house," recommends Hwangbo. For a low-carb option, try the bunless burger—same premium meat, sans bread.

2:30 P.M. WORKOUT at TAEJO KICKBOXING

552 S. Oxford Ave., Koreatown // taejokickboxing.com

The fitness options are slim in Koreatown, according to Hwangbo. "For all the eating and drinking establishments in

"Koreatown is one of the more walkable neighborhoods in Los Angeles, so you can eat dinner at a restaurant, go across the street to grab dessert and coffee, walk down the street for a drink, then head up the elevator for some karaoke and Korean bar snacks."

The Prince

K-Town, there aren't very many places to work out (unless you count all the Korean spas with fitness centers in them that no one uses). I train in Muay Thai, so thankfully there's Taejo Kickboxing nearby that I can go to when I can't make it to my home gym, CMMA Fitness."

4:30 P.M. SHOP & SNACK at THE FACE SHOP/CHOCOLATE CHAIR

621 S. Western Ave., Koreatown // international.thefaceshop.com

One of Hwangbo's favorite shops is The Face Shop, "a great store that features all the latest Korean skincare products. And after you're done buying new moisturizer

and serum, you can try a Dragon's Breath—frozen treats soaked in liquid nitrogen—from Chocolate Chair, the dessert shop connected to The Face Shop!"

7:30 P.M. FRIED CHICKEN at THE PRINCE

3198½ W. 7th St., Koreatown // theprincela.com

"It might just be the ambience of dimly lit booths and décor that hasn't been touched since it opened, but The Prince makes the best Korean-style fried chicken in town. The skin is delicately crispy and the meat is juicy and perfectly cooked," says Hwangbo of this historic

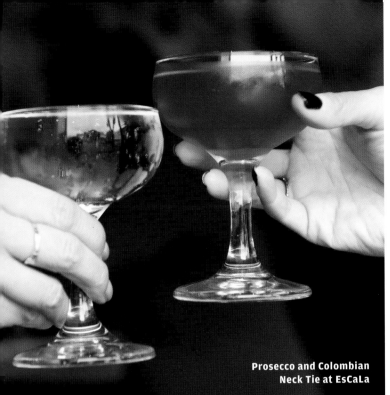

Prosecco and Colombian Neck Tie at EsCaLa

restaurant. With deep red booths and vintage lighting, The Prince has had cameos on shows from *Mad Men* to Anthony Bourdain's *The Layover*.

9:00 P.M. AFTER-DINNER DRINK at ESCALA

3451 W. 6th St., Koreatown // escalaktown.com

Hwangbo's favorite bars include Lock & Key, where she drinks the Razzle-Dazzle, a concoction of rye gin, elderflower liqueur, cucumber and rosemary, and Southland Beer for its laid-back vibe and craft beers on tap. The Colombian Neck Tie is her pick at EsCaLA. "It has a gruesome name, but the rye whiskey–based drink is smooth and not too sweet. It almost tastes like an Old Fashioned. Perfect to drink next to the floor-to-ceiling windows when they're opened onto 6th Street," she says.

ABOUT
Eunice Hwangbo is co-founder and CMO (chief marketing officer) of Zero Slant, a news and media content agency run and created by artificial intelligence. She is also a public and talent relations consultant for numerous startups and entertainment companies.

RIGHT: COURTESY EUNICE HWANGBO

MORE TO EXPLORE *KOREATOWN*

BY GRACE JIDOUN

EAT
TERRA COTTA
3760 Wilshire Blvd., Koreatown
213-365-1077 // terracottala.com
The debut of this light-filled restaurant adjoining the Art Deco Wiltern theater just made pre-show dining a lot more glamorous. Chef Danny Ye of NYC's Nobu serves craft cocktails and an international menu amid marble, plush booths and sparkling chandeliers.

EAT
POT CAFÉ AT THE LINE HOTEL
3515 Wilshire Blvd., Koreatown
213-368-3030 // eatatpot.com
This cool, minimalist café in The Line Hotel is decidedly chill, with light streaming in and a gleaming pastry case. You could come for the vibe alone, but the creative treats—from Taiwanese-style pastries to rice Kongee and horchata lattes—are also a draw.

RELAX
WI SPA
2700 Wilshire Blvd., Koreatown
213-487-2700 // wispausa.com
Five specialty saunas are just the beginning of this four-level, 24/7 relaxation emporium that incorporates many traditional features found in Korean day spas, such as a fitness room and family-friendly kid zone. Get a Korean-style body scrub or a traditional massage, then head to the restaurant before your next treatment.

EAT
TEN-RAKU
4177 W. 3rd St., Koreatown
213-380-8382 // tenrakubbq.com
Simply one of the top BBQ joints in Koreatown, Ten-Raku goes deep on what it does best, which means beautifully marbled beef, Kobe-style short ribs and other Prime cuts. But don't overlook the traditional hot pots filled with octopus and other fresh seafood.

DRINK
R BAR
3331 W. 8th St., Koreatown
213-387-7227
This password-protected speakeasy (check Facebook and Twitter) attracts one of L.A.'s cooler crowds. They come here for stiff drinks, live music, karaoke and soaking up the quirky atmosphere amid baroque chandeliers and red velvet.

WATCH
THE WILTERN
3790 Wilshire Blvd., Koreatown
213-388-1400 // wiltern.com
The stunning design of The Wiltern theater, on the ground floor of the beautiful Art Moderne Pellissier Building, is just as compelling as the musical acts who perform here. Among its most striking features are colorful murals, an Art Deco sunburst on the ceiling and a perennially packed house.

EAT
SUN HA JANG
4032 W. Olympic Blvd., Koreatown
323-634-9292
A laser focus on one ingredient—duck—sets this Korean BBQ joint apart. The casual dining room fills with smoke from tabletop grills as diners enjoy impressively flavored variations on duck Gogi Gui. The final dish: a bowl of rice upended onto the duck fat-laden griddle.

DRINK
THE WALKER INN
3612 W. 6th St., Koreatown
213-263-2709 // thewalkerinnla.com
Some of the city's most innovative cocktail creators can be found at this cozy bar behind a secret door at the back of the Normandie Lounge. Each month the imaginative drink menu is tied to a different theme.

SHOP
KOREATOWN PLAZA
928 S. Western Ave., Koreatown
213-382-1234 // koreatownplaza.com
Ground zero for funky K-Pop fashion boutiques, upscale beauty products, knickknack shops and so much more, this '80s-era mall is a full-on Seoul-inspired shopping experience. Make time to chow down in the food court, where Korean fried chicken, Vietnamese pho and Chinese dumplings are just a few of the cheap and delicious offerings.

Perry works with Joel McHale on the set of the CBS sitcom *The Great Indoors*.

CLIFF LIPSON/CBS

Blushington

Palihouse

HOLLYWOOD & LARCHMONT

Beyond the iconic tourist attractions are charming neighborhoods with trendy shops and innovative restaurants to explore. Celebrity hairstylist Jade Perry shares a few of her favorite places.

Photography by Alexander Laurent

Jade Perry lives a high-pressure Hollywood life, working with clients on film sets, photo shoots and press junkets. To balance out her hectic days on set, she spends time at the spots she loves. "I see the same faces every day," Perry says. "I frequent the same shops and restaurants and know everyone by name. We may seem to be wandering around in La La Land, but we look out for one another and we are very attached to our community."

10:30 A.M. BEAUTY BREAK at BLUSHINGTON

8591 Sunset Blvd., West Hollywood // blushington.com

For a glam squad at the ready without the sky-high cost, Perry looks to the pros at this pretty makeup studio and beauty lounge where services include eyelash extensions, brow shaping, glycolic peels and makeup application.

12:30 P.M. LUNCH at PALIHOUSE

8465 Holloway Dr., West Hollywood // palihousewesthollywood.com

The Tower Bar at Sunset Tower Hotel and The Blvd Lounge at the Beverly Wilshire are among Perry's spots for a glass of sparkling rosé, as is Palihouse with its warm, boho Lobby Lounge. Steps away from the Lobby Lounge is Mardi Restaurant, the European-inspired brasserie where locals while away brunch over polenta baked eggs and bottomless mimosas.

"The thing I love about Hollywood that I assume most people don't know is that it is an actual neighborhood."

Clare V.

Clare V. purses on display

Larchmont Village Wine, Spirits & Cheese

2:00 P.M. STYLE STOP at CLARE V.

619 N. Croft Ave., West Hollywood // clarev.com

"I'm a clutch-only type of girl, and Clare V. is the mecca of clutch bags. Her style is Parisienne chic swathed in yummy leathers. I'm obsessed," says Perry, and style bloggers and editors are, too, making Clare V. simple totes and minimalist clutches a must-have.

4:00 P.M. SHOP at LARCHMONT VILLAGE WINE, SPIRITS & CHEESE

223 N. Larchmont Blvd., Larchmont // larchmontvillagewine.com

"I wish I could live inside," Perry says. "They have a gorgeous selection of wines from just about everywhere—perfectly curated, very European and hard to find—plus a selection of cookies, crackers, oils, spices and jams. It's my first stop when planning a dinner party and my go-to when I need a great gift. Ask for Simon or Sergio, they know everything."

6:00 P.M. LIGHT SUPPER AND DRINKS at SALT'S CURE

1155 N. Highland Ave., Hollywood // saltscure.com

Perry loves the chicken liver mousse at this meat-centric bistro where chefs Chris Phelps and Zak Walters source ingredients grown and raised in California, and butcher and craft their dishes in-house.

Salt's Cure

Perry on set with Joel McHale

ABOUT

Jade Perry recently spent three months working with Donald Glover on his new FX show, *Atlanta,* all the while juggling private clients in L.A. and working out of Sally Hershberger, the eponymous salon of the highly influential hairstylist. "I constantly find myself meeting and working with people I admired and watched on television when I was younger," Perry says about her work. "I've had dinner with Olivia Newton-John and John Travolta at his house in Brentwood and chatted it up with Adriana Lima backstage at the Victoria's Secret Fashion show. My hairbrush has taken me from the White House to the tents at Bryant Park to work on every famous lot in Hollywood."

RIGHT: CLIFF LIPSON/CBS

MORE TO EXPLORE HOLLYWOOD / LARCHMONT
BY GRACE JIDOUN

EAT
PETIT TROIS

718 Highland Ave., Hollywood
323-468-8916 // petittrois.com
The unapologetically classic French fare at this casual restaurant from chef Ludo Lefebvre (of Trois Mec) will transport you to the Left Bank with one bite. The tiny storefront's no-reservations policy works for spontaneous nights out, so go ahead and satisfy those cravings for pâté de campagne and an aperitif on a whim.

EAT
MAMA SHELTER

6500 Selma Ave., Hollywood
323-785-6666 // mamashelter.com
The best way to take in the view of the Hollywood Hills? Head to the stylish rooftop of Mama Shelter, a boutique hotel near the Pantages Theatre, and grab a drink as you gaze at twinkling lights. Sip clever cocktails (the Mama Mia! blends vodka and cherry Life Savers) while working your way though shareable plates of upscale comfort food.

EAT
GWEN

6600 Sunset Blvd., Hollywood
323-946-7512 // gwenla.com
Curtis Stone presides over the Old Hollywood grandeur of this Art Deco-inspired chophouse, where the food is as ambitious as it is personal (he co-owns it with his brother, and they named it after their grandmother). Super-luxe dinners are tasting-menu only, but you can pick up charcuterie to go at the on-site butcher shop.

DRINK
25 DEGREES AND LIBRARY BAR
THE HOLLYWOOD ROOSEVELT HOTEL

7000 Hollywood Blvd., Hollywood, thehollywoodroosevelt.com
Food and booze go together deliciously at these adjacent hangouts in the historic Roosevelt Hotel. Bordello red walls set a sultry mood at 25 Degrees, where the sirloin burger is the star. For late-night drinks, head to the Library Bar, where cocktails feature seasonal ingredients of your choice.

DRINK
LOST PROPERTY BAR

1704 Vine St., Hollywood
323-987-4445 // lostpropertybar.com
David Lynch could have designed this mysterious lounge on the corner of Hollywood and Vine that's dark, moody and filled with random knickknacks that you can take home. Creative cocktails and a stellar whiskey selection draw a hip crowd that's primed to party.

WATCH
UCB THEATRE

5919 Franklin Ave., Hollywood
franklin.ucbtheatre.com
Home to the alternative comedy troupe Upright Citizens Brigade, this is the place to go for smart indie comedy. Stars from *Saturday Night Live, Parks and Recreation* and *Comedy Bang! Bang!*—as well as a grab bag of improv students— have all worked their magic on the stage.

DO
SHAPE HOUSE

434 N. Larchmont Blvd., Larchmont // 855-567-2346
shapehouse.com
Burn calories and release toxins (and exercise later) at this celebrity-favorite day spa that describes itself as an "urban sweat lodge." After relaxing in an infrared sauna bed and, yes, sweating for an hour, guests emerge renewed and refreshed.

DO
HOLLYHOCK HOUSE BARNSDALL ART PARK

4800 Hollywood Blvd., Hollywood
323-913-4030 // barnsdall.org/hollyhock-house
Built by Frank Lloyd Wright in the '20s, this National Historic Landmark, perched atop a hill in the Barnsdall Art Park, is open to the public for self-guided and docent-led tours. The textured concrete and glass structure is a spectacular example of Mayan Revival architecture.

SHOP
MELROSE PLACE

North of Melrose Ave. at La Cienega Blvd., Hollywood
Carefully curated goods for all aspects of your life can be found on this three-block stretch in West Hollywood. From Compartes Chocolatier and Alfred Coffee to boutiques like Chloé and Marc Jacobs (don't forget to check out the fine art bookshop, BookMarc, across the street), shopping here has a chic, high-end feel.

Pamela Barish

Gjusta Goods

"I ride most mornings at around 6:30 a.m. It's the most peaceful and quiet time to get around. I also love going to the marina to the little walkway that follows the harbor and watching the boats come in and go out."

VENICE

With its laid-back surfer vibe and history as an artists' community, this storied beach town has everything from eclectic shopping streets to vendor-packed boardwalks. Sculptor and painter Kristin Jai Klosterman takes us on a spin through her neighborhood.

Photography by Alexander Laurent

Although some locals decry the rapid gentrification taking place as local tech giants including Snapchat, Google and Facebook accelerate change, Venice has retained its surf-culture vibe and hip quotient. The art colony cred is authentic; Jean-Michel Basquiat, Ed Ruscha and Robert Graham (among others) all lived and worked for a time in town. Reflecting on what has drawn so many artists to Venice, Kristin Jai Klosterman says, "I love that I can walk everywhere and that it's beautiful every day. The light is fantastic. I can work outdoors in the fresh air most days."

10:30 A.M. START THE DAY at GJUSTA

320 Sunset Ave., Venice // gjusta.com

This popular bakery/deli/café serves good foods made well by chef Travis Lett. The all-day café serves everything from lox hash to smoked brisket bánh mì and, of course, freshly baked breads. Klosterman starts her day here. "I love Gjusta for breakfast. Simple bagels and juice become a perfect meal for the morning."

Gjusta

Kreation Organic Juices

12:30 P.M. SHOP FOR HOMEY TOUCHES at **GJUSTA GOODS**

324 Sunset Ave., Venice // gjustagoods.com

Housed in a 1930s art studio, the lifestyle boutique from the Gjusta/Gjelina restaurant team of Travis Lett, Fran Camaj and Shelley Armistead offers contemporary and vintage clothing, housewares, books, vinyl, and flowers for loyal fans who just can't get enough of the beloved dining spots.

1:30 P.M. RETAIL THERAPY TREAT at **PAMELA BARISH**

224 Main St., Venice // pamelabarish.com

The founder of this go-to boutique for boho-luxe pieces such as silk shirred hippie blouses and drawstring pants, Barish is also known for her line of dresses that has earned her a loyal celeb following including Anjelica Huston and Dana Delaney. Of the art-lined Main Street boutique, Klosterman says, "It's Pamela Barish for any elegant clothing I need for fancy parties or formal events."

3:00 P.M. POWER INFUSION at **KREATION ORGANIC KAFE & JUICERY**

1202 Abbot Kinney Blvd., Venice // kreationjuice.com

For a blast of raw, organic pressed juices, Klosterman stops at this juice bar and café that also serves kombuchas, mylks

Strange Invisible

and smoothies along with salads and wraps—all sourced from local farmers markets.

4:00 P.M. FIND THE PERFECT SCENT at **STRANGE INVISIBLE**

1138 Abbot Kinney Blvd., Venice // siperfumes.com

Rosamund Pike and Sophie Dahl are fans of botanical perfumer Alexandra Balahoutis and her line of limited-batch, hand-blended organic essences, all crafted in-house. The jewel-box-like boutique is a must-visit for any fragrance connoisseur.

ABOUT

Bicoastal artist Kristin Jai Klosterman creates sculptural work in metal and wood and mixed media paintings that deal with energy, environment and movement. Her large-scale metal sculptures can be found in public forums in California, Texas, Tennessee and Minnesota. Since 2006, Klosterman has been collaborating with Venice-based Light and Space artist Laddie John Dill, and has realized numerous monumental sculpture commissions all over the United States.

MORE TO EXPLORE VENICE / SANTA MONICA

BY GRACE JIDOUN

EAT
HUCKLEBERRY

1014 Wilshire Blvd., Santa Monica
310-451-2311 // huckleberrycafe.com

This charming, casual space offers a wide range of comforting baked treats and trendy breakfast dishes (we're looking at you, organic quinoa with veggies and eggs). Everything is made on-site and highlights seasonal ingredients from local farms. For a sweet snack or a full-on meal, it's hard to go wrong.

EAT
TERRAZZA AT HOTEL CASA DEL MAR

1910 Ocean Way, Santa Monica
310-581-5533 // hotelcasadelmar.com

Just off the lobby of the Hotel Casa del Mar, you'll find a transporting Mediterranean mecca, down to the blue-tiled floors, whitewashed walls and arched ceilings. But this being SoCal, the real draw is the spectacular view of the Pacific, a perfect setting for digging into Italian-inspired seafood with a craft cocktail in hand.

SHOP
LOST & FOUND

2230 Main St. // 310-450-9565
2000 Main St. // 310-450-9782
Santa Monica // lostandfoundshop.com

Japanese Shibori blankets, Ulla Johnson party dresses and Tunisian sandstone dinnerware—it's all at Lost & Found, a lifestyle boutique founded by designer Jamie Rosenthal in Hollywood. At the two shops (one for fashion, one for home), pick up unique goods from all over the world.

EAT
TACOS PUNTA CABRAS

2311 Santa Monica Blvd., Santa Monica
310-917-2244 // tacospuntacabras.com

Ask L.A. locals for their favorite taqueria and you'll get a million answers. Tacos Punta Cabras stands out for its small but mighty menu that highlights a non-GMO, sustainable philosophy. Sip on a tamarind agua fresca while waiting for Baja-style fish tacos or cocteles mixta. Most everything is made in-house.

DRINK
SHUTTERS ON THE BEACH

Living Room Lounge, 1 Pico Blvd.,
Santa Monica // 310-587-1707
shuttersonthebeach.com

Sink into one of the leather armchairs in front of the fireplace and relax with a nightcap at this cozy lounge in the posh Shutters on the Beach hotel. A view of the ocean and live music keep the mood lighthearted—a relaxing place to settle in for the evening.

SHOP
WASTELAND

1330 4th St., Santa Monica
310-395-2620 // shopwasteland.com

Wasteland is the kind of thrift store in which you can't stop scouring the racks, each time discovering a designer item at rock-bottom price. The ever-changing stock of finds ranges from vintage Chanel and Vivienne Westwood to beat-up leather jackets and chunky platforms.

EAT
SWEET ROSE CREAMERY

826 Pico Blvd., Santa Monica
310-260-2663 // sweetrosecreamery.com

This artisanal ice creamery does L.A. proud with its handcrafted ice cream made in small batches with organic, seasonal ingredients. You'll find classic flavors like old-fashioned vanilla and salted caramel, and chef's picks like guava froyo and sweet potato with salty sesame brittle, depending on what's in season.

DRINK
THE CHESTNUT CLUB

1348 14th St., Santa Monica
310-393-1348 // thechestnutclubsm.com

Santa Monica's finest cocktails are hiding in this gem across from a car dealership. Serious sippers tout the bespoke whiskey cocktails, but all of the craft drinks here are on point. Exposed brick, low lighting and a glimmering backlit bar create a cool backdrop for sipping and snacking.

DO
ANNENBERG COMMUNITY BEACH HOUSE

415 Pacific Coast Hwy.
Santa Monica // 310-458-4904
annenbergbeachhouse.com

Reserve parking ahead, then bring a group to take over the lounge chairs at this beachside public pool, once part of the ocean estate built by William Randolph Hearst for Marion Davies. The renovated complex offers a children's play area, yoga classes, gallery and café.

THE CHEFS' PICKS

Downtown L.A. spans less than six square miles, but demonstrates outsized culinary range in neighborhoods from Little Tokyo to South Park. Discover 24 favorite dishes from some of DTLA's top chefs. Incredibly, our chosen chefs gravitate toward totally different dishes.

By Joshua Lurie // Portraits by Riccardo Vecchio Imprints

Tony Esnault
Church & State, Spring

Tony Esnault grew up in rural France, developing an appreciation for produce from his grandparents. He followed a culinary path lined with Michelin stars and worked in high-end U.S. restaurants before teaming with wife Yassmin Sarmadi on two restaurants that tout ingredient-driven French cuisine.

BROKEN SPANISH'S DUCK WITH SESAME, MOLE AND PERSIMMON
"I love the depth and balance of the seasonality on this dish, and chef Ray Garcia cooks the duck just right."

KAGAYA'S SEAFOOD SHABU SHABU
"KaGaYa is a truly refined shabu shabu experience that consists of a tasting menu that changes regularly. I really like the quality, consistency and absolute freshness of the seafood in this dish every time I have it."

KINJIRO'S HOMEMADE COLD TOFU WITH CHILLED DASHI
"I love the simplicity of this dish, along with the delicate flavor of the tofu, heighted by the dashi."

L.A. CHAPTER'S FIVE LEAVES BURGER
"I really like the Five Leaves Burger by chef Ken Addington at the Ace Hotel, as it is made with dry-aged grass-fed beef, and I am a stickler about eating only 100 percent grass-fed beef. It's delicious and well seasoned, with harissa and mayonnaise, and we French love our mayo!"

PATINA'S VENISON
"Very few restaurants serve venison in Los Angeles. I love the beautiful seasonal accompaniments and the complexity of this dish, and the chef at Patina always prepares it perfectly."

Genevieve Gergis & Ori Menashe
Bestia

This culinary power couple serves as the sweet and savory engines of Bestia, a Cal-Med–influenced Italian restaurant that makes everything from scratch, including charcuterie and pasta. The exterior may be rough-hewn, but the dishes display finesse.

BROKEN SPANISH'S REFRIED LENTILS

"The refried lentils are a super-creamy, more nuanced version of classic refried beans."

FRITZI'S BEEF BURGER

"Just a really good, flavorful burger."

MANUELA'S CORNMEAL PANCAKES WITH PRESERVED PEACHES

"Really great buttery, crisp-edged pancakes with melted butter and real maple syrup."

SUSHI GEN'S TORO SUSHI

"They always have both medium and fatty toro, and the quality of both are always super high for a decent price and pretty good portion size."

WEXLER'S DELI'S SMOKED STURGEON AND CREAM CHEESE BAGEL

"The sturgeon has a great texture and just the right amount of smoke."

BÄCO MERCAT
408 S. Main St., Historic Core
213-687-8808 // bacomercat.com

BAR AMÁ
118 W. 4th St., Historic Core
213-687-8002 // bar-ama.com

BESTIA
2121 E. 7th Pl., Arts District
213-514-5724 // bestiala.com

BROKEN SPANISH
1050 S. Flower St., South Park
213-749-1460 // brokenspanish.com

CHURCH & STATE
1850 Industrial St., Arts District
213-405-1434 // churchandstatebistro.com

DANNY'S TACOS (food truck)
1023 S. Grand Ave., South Park
323-529-7486

EVERSON ROYCE BAR
1936 E. 7th St., Arts District
213-335-6166 // erbla.com

FRITZI
814 Traction Ave., Arts District
213-537-0327 // fritzidtla.com

KAGAYA
418 E. 2nd St., Little Tokyo
213-617-1016

KAZUNORI
421 S. Main St., Historic Core
213-493-6956 // kazunorisushi.com

KINJIRO
424 E. 2nd St., Little Tokyo
213-229-8200 // kinjiro-la.com

L.A. CHAPTER
927 S. Broadway, Fashion District
213-235-9660 // lachapter.com

LEDLOW
400 S. Main St., Historic Core
213-687-7015 // ledlowla.com

MANUELA Hauser Wirth & Schimmel
907 E. 3rd St., Arts District
323-849-0480 // manuela-la.com

MARUGAME MONZO
329 E. 1st St., Little Tokyo
213-346-9762 // marugamemonzo.com

ORSA & WINSTON
122 W. 4th St., Historic Core
213-687-0300 // orsaandwinston.com

OTIUM
222 S. Hope St., Bunker Hill
213-935-8500 // otiumla.com

PACIFIC DINING CAR
1310 W. 6th St., West Lake (just outside 110)
213-483-6000 // pacificdiningcar.com

PATINA
141 S. Grand Ave., Bunker Hill
213-972-3331 // patinarestaurant.com

P.Y.T.
400 S. Main St., Historic Core
213-687-7015 // pytlosangeles.com

RICEBAR
419 7th St., Financial District
213-807-5341 // ricebarla.com

SHIBUMI
815 S. Hill St., South Park
213-265-7923 // shibumidtla.com

SONORATOWN
208 E. 8th St., Fashion District
213-290-5184 // sonoratownla.com

SPRING
257 S. Spring St., Historic Core
213-372-5189 // springlosangeles.com

SUSHI GEN
422 E. 2nd St., Little Tokyo
213-617-0552 // sushigen-dtla.com

WEXLER'S DELI Grand Central Market
317 S. Broadway, Historic Core
213-620-0633 // wexlersdeli.com

ZINC CAFÉ
580 Mateo St., Arts District
323-825-5381 // zinccafe.com

Josef Centeno
Bäco Mercat, Bar Amá, Ledlow,
Orsa & Winston, P.Y.T.

Josef Centeno worked for fine-dining restaurants in New York City and Northern California before developing a signature style that fuses comfort food with seasonal ingredients at his growing empire in the Old Bank District.

Timothy Hollingsworth
Otium

Timothy Hollingsworth trained under Thomas Keller for years at The French Laundry before opening grand, globally inspired Otium in the shadow of The Broad museum and the smoke-fueled Barrel & Ashes barbecue restaurant in Studio City.

BESTIA'S VEAL TARTARE
"You don't get veal tartare everywhere; it's really great with the tonnato sauce, a classical pairing with veal. The tartare here comes with a side of grilled bread, which is one of my favorite things, and really completes the dish."

BROKEN SPANISH'S PORK CHICHARRÓN
"When I ordered this dish the first time, I wasn't really sure what to expect, and it was just so good. It has a perfect balance with acidity and the richness of the pork."

David Schlosser
Shibumi

David Schlosser trained in Japan and applies those lessons in DTLA at Shibumi, a refined kappo-style restaurant that presents seasonal ingredients on handmade ceramics at a counter crafted from 400-year-old cypress.

EVERSON ROYCE BAR'S TOKEN FRENCHIE SALAD

"The token Frenchie salad is a nice surprise for a bar menu, and I always get it before I eat the burger and biscuits."

KAGAYA'S BEEF SHABU SHABU

"The beef shabu shabu is what dreams are made of."

PACIFIC DINING CAR'S COWBOY STEAK

"The cowboy and a chocolate soufflé, followed by a bone-dry martini. Need I say more?"

RICEBAR'S PORK LONGGANISA

"Charles [Olalia]'s pork longganisa has so much flavor and is a true comfort dish."

DANNY'S TACOS' MULITAS

"When you're in the restaurant industry, a lot of times you get out of work really late. Taco trucks make for great places for late-night meals. The mulitas at Danny's are my go-to."

MARUGAME MONZO'S VONGOLE

"I've had vongole plenty of times, but never with udon. Plus, the fact that you're sitting there in front of the person actually making the noodles is awesome."

SUSHI GEN'S ANKIMO

"I really love monkfish liver, and not a lot of sushi places usually have it. Gen's preparation is great; it's delicate and balanced with the sweetness of ponzu and sharpness of scallions."

BESTIA'S MARGHERITA PIZZA

"The philosophy of the pizza is great. Ori [Menashe] is doing a couple of things, using wild yeast to make the dough; he's also using a wood-fired oven…. There's a lot of character in the pizza and you can taste the efforts."

KAZUNORI'S HAND ROLLS

"Really high-quality nori; the rice is warm and cooked well; and the fish is fresh and cleanly sliced. Just those three things, very simple. They're doing 400 to 500 guests per day, and there are only 22 seats, so they're doing something right."

SONORATOWN'S SONORAN BURRITOS

"Sonora, Mexico, is the region where the burrito was invented. We in California are used to these giant burritos with tons of fillings; you need two hands to hold them. Burritos are supposed to be little snacks…. We change things a lot in L.A. because of fusion cuisine, but they're showing what burritos should be."

WEXLER'S DELI'S PASTRAMI SANDWICH

"Being an aficionado of pastrami sandwiches, which I take very seriously, I think it's done very well. I like the bread, I like the meat and I like the mustard."

ZINC CAFÉ'S SALAD

"This one's probably more about the vibe, the environment. The salads are good and there's a sense of community at Zinc. It's good vegetables, done well."

Bestia

FLYING HIGH
REDBIRD
114 E. 2nd St. // 213-788-1191
redbird.la

Located inside the rectory of a former cathedral (also one of L.A.'s oldest buildings), Redbird is a decadent dining experience by Neal Fraser, from the "amuse-booze" that greets guests upon sitting to the highly skilled technique on display in the menu's "New American" highlights.

PARDON MY FRENCH
SPRING
257 S. Spring St. // 213-372-5189
springlosangeles.com

It may not have the most inventive name, but this eatery—a spacious, light-filled dining room sporting a fountain, plenty of greenery and an open kitchen—offers refined dishes recalling the South of France, from pâtes and escargots to classically prepared meats and fish.

PAR FOR THE COURSE
ORSA & WINSTON
122 W. 4th St. // 213-687-0300
orsaandwinston.com

Known for its tasting menus—offered in four, five, nine or 20 small courses—Orsa & Winston's artfully plated dishes span the gamut of flavors, from Spanish to French to Italian to Asian. It's a small restaurant, with only 33 seats, so reservations (preferably near the open kitchen) are recommended.

HAVE FAITH (AND ABSINTHE)
FAITH & FLOWER
705 W. 9th St. // 213-239-0642
faithandflowerla.com

Offering opulent takes on New American cuisine, this Art Deco-tinged spot draws a trendy crowd with an inventive menu and Roaring '20s-inspired cocktail program. The raw bar offers chilled seafood delights, while the Absinthe menu sets it apart from other Downtown mainstays.

DISTRICT BOOK
OUR FAVES
EAT
DTLA

FINE DINING

BELLY OF THE BEAST
BESTIA
2121 E. 7th Pl. // 213-514-5724
bestiala.com

A shining star of Downtown L.A.'s dining scene, Bestia serves up creative multi-regional Italian dishes (pastas, pizzas, cured meats among them) in a hyper-masculine, loud, industrial space. (Note the meathook chandeliers.) Just be sure to make your reservations far in advance.

THE MEAT OF THE MATTER
OFFICINE BRERA
1331 E. 6th St. // 213-553-8006
officinebrera.com

Located in a massive Arts District warehouse, this sleek and sophisticated spot is straight out of Northern Italy, serving up hearty meat dishes, homemade pastas and a few seafood standouts. Ask about the off-menu farinata, a chickpea pancake that draws raves from diners.

Redbird

FOOD AS AN ARTFORM
PATINA

141 S. Grand Ave. // 213-972-3331
patinarestaurant.com

Sure, having dinner at this Michelin-starred spot—located inside the Walt Disney Concert Hall—will set you back a paycheck, but Patina's incomparable sophistication, unmatched service and its highly skilled and artfully plated dishes are how you know it's worth it.

VIEW FROM THE TOP
71 ABOVE

633 W. 5th St., 71st Floor // 213-712-2683
71above.com

The ultimate date night spot, no restaurant in California offers the 360-degree view obtainable here, high atop the US Bank Tower. Chef Vartan Abgaryan serves artfully composed dishes, with the $70 three-course option your best bet for a perfectly crafted experience.

71 Above

DISTRICT

Bold Flavors Meet Urban Sophistication

Let your senses be dazzled by Chef Hansen Lee's modern, approachable menu inspired by the extraordinary sustainably-grown ingredients purveyed by local farmers. Each dish pairs perfectly with the bar's enticing hand-crafted cocktails. At DISTRICT not only do we make use of the extraordinary foods grown sustainably by our local farmers, we also seek out unparalleled ideas from food purveyors around the world.

Reservations can be made via www.districtdtla.com or by calling 213 612 3185.

District is located within the Bloc • 711 South Hope Street, Los Angeles, CA 9001

Sticky Rice

Knead & Co.

GRAND CENTRAL MARKET
317 S. Broadway, Historic Core // grandcentralmarket.com

Located in the heart of Downtown at Broadway and 3rd Street, this local landmark is a perfect showcase of L.A.'s various cultures and cuisines

BECAUSE VEGETABLES
MADCAPRA

This local spot by Brooklyn chefs Sarah Hymanson and Sara Kramer consistently receives rave reviews for its falafel-based menu. A favorite spot among vegetarians, vegans and meat-lovers alike, you'd be hard-pressed to find tastier Middle Eastern delights in Los Angeles.

EGG ON (AND IN) YOUR FACE
EGGSLUT

This place is a breakfast phenomenon, as evidenced by the mile-long line leading to the counter each and every morning. Open 'til 4 p.m., Eggslut reworks the simplest of ingredients, the egg, into downright delicious creations. Arrive early to enjoy a house-made buttermilk biscuit.

Eggslut

MARKET: POUL LANGE; STICKY RICE: AMPARO RIOS; EGGSLUT: JAKOB LAYMAN; KNEAD & CO.: MARIE BUCK

THE MEAT EXPERTS
BELCAMPO MEAT CO.

More than a full-service butcher shop (serving only locally raised, organic, grass-fed meats), Belcampo serves up five variations of a mouth-watering burger (including one for vegetarians) in a retro-modern diner with counter service, complete with beer and wine.

WHAT'S THE SCOOP?
McCONNELL'S FINE ICE CREAMS

This Santa Barbara ice cream institution has been around for decades, treating locals to small batches of inventive flavors, made with dairy from its own creamery and a slew of local organic ingredients from partner farms. You won't find a scoop as smooth as these in all of Downtown.

CHARMING CONFECTIONS
VALERIE CONFECTIONS BAKERY & CAFÉ

Step up to the counter of this coffee shop and bakery for sandwiches, salads and other brunch standards, but don't leave without treating yourself to Valerie's pastries and desserts (croissants, hand pies, petits fours, cakes and chocolates), perfect for any time of day.

A TASTE OF ITALY
KNEAD & CO.

This pasta bar and market offers up Northern Italian dishes, all made from scratch. Stop by in the morning for a breakfast sandwich, or satisfy your need for homemade pasta with the Sunday Gravy Spaghetti & Meatballs, just as hearty and delicious as your nonna used to make.

ALL THAI'D UP
STICKY RICE

Dedicated to delicious Thai comfort food, the menu at Grand Central Market's Sticky Rice—seasonal and created with local ingredients in mind—offers up flavorful, authentic dishes (the Hainan Chicken and Beef Panang being standouts) as well as those popular Thai plates you know and love.

JEWISH SOUL FOOD
WEXLER'S DELI

L.A. chef Micah Wexler started this nouveau-traditional Jewish deli back in 2014, and ever since he's dedicated himself to serving old-school dishes—smoked meat and fish (done in-house on the daily), bagels and egg creams being the stars of the show.

Wexler's Deli

SMORGASBURG L.A.

Sea Urchin, The Jolly Oyster

Lobsterdamus

Better than the Brooklyn Original

777 Alameda St., Industrial District // la.smorgasburg.com

Sorry, NYC, but when it comes to outdoor markets, L.A.'s got your number. The Brooklyn-born food market that began as a spinoff of Brooklyn Flea has found a happy home at the Row. Every Sunday from 10 a.m. – 4 p.m. (hours vary by season), you'll find an amazing lineup of 75+ food and shopping vendors. It's the perfect place to discover up-and-coming businesses and restaurants. Some standouts include Amazebowls, Porridge and Puffs, Mama Musubi and Lobsterdamus—just to name a few. Smorgasburg L.A. seems to draw a more eclectic crowd than its New York counterpart, which can be attributed to its adventurous food vendors as well as its prime location Downtown. Foodies flock here by the dozen to end their week on a high note with mom-and-pop shop arepas, pizza, tacos, homemade popsicles and more. And why wouldn't they? The brand-new parking structure (785 Bay St.) fits up to 5,000 cars and is free for the first two hours—pretty much unheard of Downtown. Follow @smorgasburgla for updates and special event announcements (think Pie Day and holiday markets). —*Lydia Mack*

BURGERS

Belcampo Meat Co.

BURGERS GONE BONKERS
THE ESCONDITE
410 Boyd St. // 213-626-1800
theescondite.com

The burgers at this local hideout are incomparable in their imaginative flavor combinations. Options like the "Fat Albert" (provolone, bacon and maple syrup, on a glazed donut bun) give you a sense of the off-the-wall meal that awaits you.

FUSION FAVORITE
CHAYA
525 S. Flower St. // 213-236-9577
thechaya.com

While a French-Japanese fusion restaurant may seem like the last place that would make a killer burger, Chaya proves just the opposite. The all-American classic gets Chef Joji Inoue's treatment, which is sure to impress. Consider yourself lucky if the wagyu beef burger is on the menu.

ON THE (BUTCHER) BLOCK
BELCAMPO MEAT CO.
317 S. Broadway // 213-625-0304
belcampo.com

When it comes to beef, no one does it better than this full-service butcher shop found inside Downtown's Grand Central Market. Head here for five variations on a classic burger, including a turkey burger, lamb burger and veggie option.

SIMPLE YET SOPHISTICATED
EVERSON ROYCE BAR
1936 E. 7th St. // 213-335-6166
erbla.com

A popular bar among the young and hip, E.R.B. doubles as a local favorite for casual but sophisticated eats on the spacious ooutdoor patio. The kitchen is open late, allowing you to order up a burger (traditional or grilled pork chorizo) til 1 a.m.

AHOY! BURGERS AHEAD!
REDWOOD BAR & GRILL
316 W. 2nd St. // 213-680-2600
theredwoodbar.com

It's hard to believe that a 'bar in a sunken pirate ship' concept could be popular for anything but its wacky décor, but this popular spot for pub grub and live music is beloved for its classic burger, made with half a pound of grilled Angus.

THE BOMBAY BURGER
BADMAASH
108 W. 2nd St. // 213-221-7466
badmaashla.com

You might not think to hit up an Indian gastropub for a great burger, but this place specializes in street eats, and the lamb burger—ground and spiced in-house daily, served with paprika-spiced mayo on brioche—is a favorite.

COZY COCKTAILS
LIBRARY BAR
630 W. 6th St. // 213-614-0053
librarybarla.com

Many have called this spot's Library Burger the best burger in all of L.A. Those are fighting words in a city that birthed burger greats like Father's Office and Umami, but even so, Library Bar's burger (and fries!) stand up to the competition.

JAKOB LAYMAN

BREAKFAST, BRUNCH & LUNCH

L.A. Chapter

Pitchoun Bakery & Café

COUNT YOUR CHANGE
NICKEL DINER
524 S. Main St. // 213-623-8301
nickeldiner.com

This diner with a vintage tinge serves up all the old-school dishes you crave. Show up early for breakfast—both to get a seat and to get your hands on the maple bacon donut that put this place on the map. Later in the day, opt for a slice of one of the Nickel's many gorgeous desserts.

A TASTE OF SOUTHERN FRANCE
PITCHOUN BAKERY & CAFÉ
545 S. Olive St. // 213-689-3240
pitchounbakery.com

The pastry shop of your dreams, Pitchoun (an affectionate term meaning "kiddo" in French) offers traditional salads, sandwiches and soups, though most are entranced by the selection of artisan breads, pastries and cakes. Best of all, everything is made in-house daily.

FOR THE HIP HOTEL SET
L.A. CHAPTER
927 S. Broadway // 213-235-9660
lachapter.com

Located on the ground floor of Downtown's beloved Ace Hotel, the black-and-white checkered floors of this French bistro beckon the city's hipsters and foodies. Start your day with ricotta pancakes, avocado toast and a 10-ingredient (as it should be) Bloody Mary.

DOWNTOWN'S COUNTRY CAFE
POPPY & ROSE
765 Wall St. // 213-995-7799
poppyandrosela.com

Known for its chicken and waffles, biscuits and gravy and other American comfort food dishes, this casual spot in the Flower District (open as early as 6 a.m. and serving breakfast, lunch and brunch 'til 3) takes its inspiration from a Southern country kitchen.

A BUNCH OF BRUNCH OPTIONS
BRUNCHDTLA
718 S. Los Angeles St. // 213-944-8326

Located inside a small food court, BrunchDTLA is known for an extensive selection of reasonably priced fusion dishes (Thai and Korean among them) and for its large portions. The bibimbap breakfast burrito is a local favorite, as are the waffles, served with creative toppings.

CLASSIC & COMFORTABLE
LEDLOW
400 S. Main St. // 213-687-7015
ledlowla.com

Considered to be one of L.A.'s essential brunch spots, this hyped-up, minimalist "ode to the American diner" serves up generously sized plates of down-home comfort food (with a twist, courtesy of chef Josef Centeno). In perfect weather, the sidewalk patio beckons.

JUST A LITTLE FRENCH
LE PETIT PARIS
418 S. Spring St. // 213-217-4445
lepetitparisla.com

Hailing from Cannes, restaurateurs David and Fanny Rolland opened this elegant two-story brasserie back in 2015. While it's great for date night, it's also a beloved brunch spot, when classic French dishes are served up and mimosas flow freely.

GOURMET MEXICAN

ALL FLAVOR, NO BULL
B.S. TAQUERIA
514 W. 7th St. // 213-622-3744
bstaqueria.com

The younger brother of Ray Garcia's Broken Spanish, the emphasis here is on whimsical Mexican-fusion street eats. Foodies have long raved over the clams-and-lardo tacos and the spicy mixed seafood ceviche. The tres leches cake is also a sweet favorite.

FRESHNESS FIRST
TABACHINES COCINA
517 S. Spring St. // 213-489-2950
tabachinescocina.com

If your idea of Mexican eats includes rice and beans slathered with melted cheese, you're in for a surprise at Tabachines, where the dishes are bold, bright and use only the freshest of ingredients. (Dare we say it's even healthy?) Ceviche, salads, seafood and mole rule the menu.

TEX-MEX DONE RIGHT
BAR AMÁ
118 W. 4th St. // 213-687-8002
bar-ama.com

It's not easy to find Tex-Mex eats in Southern California, but this local cantina serves it up skillfully. Order up down-home dishes like the chips and queso (add chorizo for a little extra spice), Frito pie, fajitas and enchiladas, accompanied with a tequila cocktail or cerveza.

THE BADDEST
MÁS MALO
515 W. 7th St. // 213-985-4332
masmalorestaurant.com

An energetic spot serving upscale comida and a wide-ranging list of tequilas and mezcal (nearly 300), Más Malo showcases Chef Robert Luna's take on East L.A.-style Chicano dishes, both classic and with a twist. Come for the finely crafted dishes and cocktails, stay for the scene.

NO LANGUAGE BARRIER HERE
BROKEN SPANISH
1050 S. Flower St. // 213-749-1460
brokenspanish.com

Chef Ray Garcia has piled up the accolades for this take on modern Mexican cuisine, deftly balancing home-cooked comfort food with skillful fine dining. The bright space, filled with Mexican pottery and colorful tiles, is an ideal setting for Garcia's inventive throwback dishes.

THE COAST IS CLEAR
PEZ CANTINA
401 S. Grand Ave. // 213-258-2280
pezcantina.com

The focus at chef-owner Bret Thompson's vibrant Mexican spot is on freshly grilled coastal cuisine, with inspirational cues taken from the Yucatan, Baja and Oaxacan regions of the country. A playful cocktail program round out classic dishes—tacos, coctels and salads among them.

B.S. Taqueria

Pez Cantina

Sonoratown

TACOS

LIKE THEY DO UP NORTH
SONORATOWN
208 E. 8th St. // 213-290-5184 // sonoratownla.com

Specializing in Northern Mexican (Sonora-style) dishes, pop into this small 12-seater storefront for traditional carne asada tacos on fresh-made flour tortillas (not the corn tortillas favored by other local spots). The chimichangas and quesadillas are well-crafted guest stars—as is the Lorenza, which is basically a crunchy Mexican pizza—and you'll want to wash down your meal with an agua fresca, of which three types are typically for sale.

FRESH FACE
GUERILLA TACOS
323-388-5340 // guerillatacos.com

With California and French influences, Chef Wes Avila is a man of the people. His tacos are unpretentious but full of flavor, guaranteed to impress. His ingredients are locally sourced, and the ever-changing menu is never dull. Check out Guerilla's website, because this food truck is on the move daily.

ONE HOT CHICA
CHICA'S TACOS
728 S. Olive St. // 213-896-0373 // chicastacos.com

It may be a tiny little shack at only 700 square feet, but these tacos are big on flavor. Choose from five variations (steak, chicken, pork, fish and veggie) before grabbing your (quite hefty) meal, stopping over at the salsa bar and grabbing a seat at a communal picnic table out back.

ONLY A BUCK
CASA LA DOÑA
800 S. Main St. // 213-627-7441

When you're craving flavorful Mexican, head to this casa, where the tacos are served on homemade corn tortillas and on a Tuesday will only set you back one dollar (tortillas will be pre-made). Look out for their extensive salsa selection for an extra bonus.

HOMEY & HANDMADE
GUISADOS
541 S. Spring St. // 213-627-7656 // guisados.co

This local chain is considered the gold standard of tacos by many an Angeleno, and its Downtown outlet is a great spot for simple tacos (on corn tortillas) made with traditional fillings, from chicharron to steak picado to veggie options. Can't decide? Order the six-mini-taco sampler.

POUL LANGE

LATE-NIGHT EATS

MOONLIGHT BITES
BÄCO MERCAT
408 S. Main St. // 213-687-8808
bacomercat.com

The late-night happy hour at this hopping neighborhood spot (served at the bar and on the patio, 10 p.m. to close during the week, 11 p.m. to close on weekends) offers great deals on favorite food and drink items, like the bäco, a flatbread that combines the best aspects of pizza, tacos and gyros.

AROUND THE CLOCK
24/7 AT THE STANDARD
550 S. Flower St. // 213-439-3030
standardhotels.com

Popular among hotel guests and post-party Downtown revelers, this diner-ish spot inside the Standard Hotel serves comfort food all day long without closing. If you're solo, grab a spot at the counter, or park yourself outside on the patio if you've got a large group in tow.

THE HOT DOG, ELEVATED
WURSTKÜCHE
800 E. 3rd St. // 213-687-4444
wurstkuche.com

Open 'til 1:30 a.m. every night of the week, Wurstküche is Downtown's go-to spot for sausages (served on fresh rolls with a variety of toppings and gourmet mustards) and Belgian fries. If you're feeling adventurous, the exotic sausages are what you've been looking for.

A SLICE AND A MOVIE
PELLICOLA PIZZERIA
421 W. 8th St. // 213-614-8000
213dthospitality.com

Pellicola's pizza combines New York-style crunch with Neapolitan-style lightness, and it's open 'til 3 a.m. on weekends (11 p.m. during the week). Stop by for movie night on Tuesdays and Wednesdays. (Check the restaurant's Instagram for the weekly movie lineup.)

Bäco Mercat

BREAKFAST FOR DINNER
WAKE & LATE
105 E. 6th St. // 213-537-0820
wakeandlate.com

Whether you're an early bird or a night owl known to sleep through breakfast, this delivery and eat-in spot gives you the freedom to choose, at affordable prices. They're open super early and super late, so stop in or schedule your delivery ahead of time.

HITTING THE SWEET SPOT
BIRDIES
314 W. Olympic Blvd. // 213-536-5720
birdiesla.com

Part-coffee, part-donuts, part-fried chicken, Birdies (open 24 hours on Friday and Saturday) is the perfect solution to late-night cravings. The original chicken sandwich is crisp and juicy, while the made-on-the-hour artisanal donuts come in a slew of inventive flavors.

COOKING WITH SOUL
COMFORT L.A.
1110 E. 7th St. // 213-537-0844
comfortla.net

This spot doesn't close its doors until 3 a.m. on Fridays and Saturdays, perfect for the late-night bar-hopping crowd. You won't find better or more authentic soul food in all of Downtown, and you can taste the love in the fried chicken, greens and mac 'n' cheese.

ALWAYS OPEN
THE ORIGINAL PANTRY CAFE
877 S. Figueroa St. // 213-972-9279
pantrycafe.com

In the mood for a little nostalgia? Rumor has it this nearly 100-year-old diner doesn't even have a lock on the door due to its 24/7 schedule. Step in for an old-school plate of steak and eggs or a couple massive pancakes, perfect for a late-night bite.

AMERICAN EATS
L.A. CAFÉ
639 S. Spring St. // 213-612-3000
thelacafe.com

A full page of the menu at this simple 24-hour counter-service spot is dedicated to that most perfect of entrées—the burger— from the simplest of chuck burgers to the Japanese-tinged Dojo Burger, served with red ginger, tonkatsu sauce and wasabi mayo.

UNDER THE SEA
FULLHOUSE SEAFOOD
963 N. Hill St. // 213-617-8382
lafullhouserestaurant.com

Open every day 'til 3 a.m., this local spot is packed late-night with those seeking authentic Chinese dishes. The place itself has a rich history, opened in 1982, and it hasn't stopped serving some of the city's best Chinese since. A true local gem.

DYLAN + JENI

FRIED CHICKEN

Poppy & Rose

GET READY TO SWEAT
HOWLIN' RAY'S
727 N. Broadway #128 // 213-935-8399
howlinrays.com

Step up to the counter at this tiny Chinatown stripmall spot for (who knew?) authentic Nashville-style hot fried chicken, a foodie trend that even KFC has attempted to capitalize on. You'll pick from six spice levels, but only daredevils should attempt the truly spicy stuff.

LIKE GRANDMA MAKES
POPPY & ROSE
765 Wall St. // 213-995-7799
poppyandrosela.com

This place is known for comfort food, which includes its signature buttermilk fried chicken and a waffle, accompanied by smoked honey butter and chives. (Is your mouth watering yet?) Prepare to be transported to your granny's Southern kitchen.

Howlin' Ray's

THESE BIRDS HAVE SOUL
COMFORT L.A.
1110 E. 7th St. // 213-537-0844
comfortla.net

The go-to spot for soul food Downtown, you can't go wrong with Comfort's dinner special, consisting of five fried chicken wings, a piece of cornbread and two sides, from which you can choose collard greens, mac 'n' cheese and more. Heaven.

SWEET TALKER
BIRDIES
314 W. Olympic Blvd. // 213-536-5720
birdiesla.com

If you're seeking something sweet to accompany that fried bird craving, look no further. Order up a chicken sandwich (topped with cole slaw, cheddar, pickle and buttermilk ranch mayo), or an old-fashioned breast and wing. Just leave room for the homemade donuts.

UPSCALE BIRD
LEDLOW
400 S. Main St. // 213-687-7015
ledlowla.com

One of Downtown's more costly spots for finger-licking fried chicken, Ledlow is popular among the hipster set for its comfort food dishes with creative twists. Monday night is Spicy Fried Chicken Night, where you'll drop coin for a full bird, best enjoyed on the outdoor patio.

FRIED AND TRUE
SIXTH STREET TAVERN
630 W. 6th St. // (213) 614-1900
sixthstreettavern.com

You can't hit this popular gastropub and not try its signature chicken and donuts. What you get is three pieces of chicken, fried to perfection, served atop donuts fried in the same oil to absorb the flavor. Believe the hype—somehow it's a winning combo.

Peking Tavern

SWEET AND SAVORY TREATS
CRÊPES SANS FRONTIERES
541 S. Spring St. // 213-623-3606
crepessansfrontieres.com

Tucked away in the Spring Street Arcade Building, Crêpes Sans Frontieres is a stylish spot that serves fanciful sweet and savory crêpe creations (with gluten-free options, to boot), in addition to charcuterie plates, delicious toasts and wines. Note, though, that it's closed on Mondays.

FAST-CASUAL FILIPINO
RICEBAR
419 W. 7th St. // 213-807-5341
ricebarla.com

Downtown's go-to Filipino restaurant serves up modern takes on classic comfort dishes. Seating is extremely limited at this fast-casual spot (with only seven seats at the kitchen-facing counter), where you'll craft a rice bowl from imported ingredients and traditional Filipino flavors.

A TRIP TO THAILAND
POK POK L.A.
978 N. Broadway // 213-613-1831
pokpokla.com

Portland chef Andy Ricker is world-famous for his über-traditional and skillful take on Thai dishes. Once here, you can't go wrong with the Pok Pok Special: half a roasted chicken and papaya salad, the first two dishes Ricker ever served at Pok Pok's original location.

WELCOME TO N'AWLINS
PREUX & PROPER
840 S. Spring St. // 213-896-0090
preuxandproper.com

For the Southern delicacies of New Orleans (po' boys, catfish, jambalaya, étouffée), head to this open-air patio spot that serves frozen daiquiris downstairs. Whether you're seeking the hedonism of Bourbon Street or the refined beauty of the Garden District, you'll find it here.

DISTRICT BOOK
OUR FAVES
EAT
DTLA

BACK TO BEIJING
PEKING TAVERN
806 S. Spring St. // 213-988-8308 // pekingtavern.com

It's often said this underground gastropub (enter off the street and head downstairs) has a '90s Beijing vibe, and Peking Tavern is indeed known for serving up street-style dishes, from its delectable Sichuan fish dumplings (the red oil garlic sauce produces a numbing sensation) and hand-pulled noodles (made on-site in a glass-walled kitchen) to other flavorful eats. In addition to a cocktail program and craft beer, it's also the only place in town that serves up Chinese Baiju cocktails.

BRAZILIAN HOME COOKING
WOODSPOON
107 W. 9th St. // 213-629-1765 // woodspoonla.com

You've likely never had Brazilian food like this, inspired by the country's African, European and Indian influences, served in an intimate 'shabby chic' environment. WoodSpoon isn't a Brazilian steakhouse, instead serving traditional street food, like its signature dish, which is reminiscent of chicken pot pie.

EMI ROSE KITAWAKI

Badmaash, Mezzanine level

Badmaash

EMI ROSE KITAWAKI

TRULY BADASS
BADMAASH
108 W. 2nd St. // 213-221-7466 // badmaashla.com

The menu at this beloved Downtown spot (the name is Hindu for "badass") reflects its owners' Indian heritage and Canadian upbringing. Customers fall in love with the fused flavors of dishes like the Chicken Tikka Poutine, while a Bollywood-meets-Warhol design beckons a young, hip clientele.

HEAVEN FOR CARNIVORES
1810
105 W. 9th St. // 213-623-1810
1810restaurant.com

A sleek and modern white-bricked space serving meat-centric Argentinian food, 1810 transports diners to South America. Order traditional starters like empanadas and croquetas, then splurge on the Parrillada Mixta, a massive platter of six different meats.

LIKE THEY DO DOWN UNDER
BRONZED AUSSIE
714 S. Los Angeles St. // 213-243-0770
bronzedaussie.us

A revelation when it popped up Downtown in 2013, this bakery/coffee shop serves up crisp, golden hand pies, both sweet and savory. For a real treat, stop in for breakfast (or brekkie, as the Aussies say) and lose yourself in the flavors of a bacon, sausage and egg pie.

FRESH VIETNAMESE
BLOSSOM RESTAURANT
426 S. Main St. // 213-623-1973
blossomrestaurant.com

Sit inside or on the sidewalk of this popular Vietnamese spot to enjoy pho and other regional dishes. The restaurant itself is sleek and modern, a nice juxtaposition with its traditional take on healthy, Saigon-style food. Blossom's sophisticated wine list is an added bonus.

BAO DOWN
THE CHAIRMAN
1200 E. 5th St. // 213-289-9808
hailthechairman.com

The bao game is strong at this San Francisco food truck-turned-restaurant in the Arts District. Striking the right balance of fluffy and soft, these baos are the perfect vehicle to deliver flavorful meats like brisket and Coca-Cola-braised pork.

VIET IT
LITTLE SISTER
523 W. 7th St. // 213-628-3146
littlesisterla.com

In a city riddled with pho restaurants, Little Sister offers a break from the norm with contemporary Vietnamese cuisine. While Little Sister bills itself as "East-meets-West inspired dishes," the *L.A. Times*' Jonathan Gold has dubbed Chef Vuong's style "anti-fusion cooking." Expect modern dishes with traditional flavors.

Church and State

THE TRUE FRENCH BISTRO
CHURCH AND STATE
1850 Industrial St. // 213-405-1434 // churchandstatebistro.com

This bistro serves up a variety of French dishes and wines, but it's hard to top its French fries, served with aioli, even better when accompanied by the grass-fed flat iron steak.

GET SAUCY
CENTO
128 E. 6th St. // 213-489-0131
centopasta.com

When that craving for handmade pasta hits (and it will), Chef Avner Lavi's got you covered at his lunch-only pop-up located inside Mignon. The former Bestia chef cooks up handmade pastas and sauces for diners without that Bestia budget, and delivers the dishes of the day verbally, so you won't need a printed menu.

GAME TIME TAPAS
CLEO
800 W. Olympic Blvd.
424-888-7818 // sbe.com/cleolalive

The L.A. Live outpost of SBE's Cleo brings a refreshing alternative to burgers and beer that dominates your pre- and post-Lakers game dining options. The modern twist on Mediterranean small plates features must-order items like the pork belly kebab and lamb sliders.

HAPPY HOUR

GET POWERED UP
THE EDISON
108 W. 2nd St. // 213-613-0000
edisondowntown.com

Take in a live band—or a silent movie projected onto the walls—while enjoying inexpensive apps and reduced-price beer, wine and cocktails, every Wednesday, Thursday and Friday (5-7 p.m.) at this steampunk-meets-Art Nouveau spot, formerly L.A.'s very first power plant.

DON'T HAVE A COW
BLUE COW KITCHEN
350 S. Grand Ave. // 213-621-2249
bluecowkitchen.com

Offering $6 cocktails, wines and sangria margaritas, happy hour here (4-6:30 p.m. on weekdays) is a guaranteed good time. Popular among those who work nearby, Blue Cow offers a ton of delicious small bites and a casual patio area in the middle of Downtown.

NO PLACE LIKE HOME
ARTISAN HOUSE
600 S. Main St. // 213-622-6333
artisanhouse.net

This restaurant, bar and on-site market offers a $5 happy hour (cocktails, wine and draft beer) from 3-7 p.m. on weekdays. Share plates—from pizza and sliders to its popular Red Thai Curry Mussels—are also served up in the bar area's industrial-chic surroundings.

THERE GOES THE NEIGHBORHOOD
THE STOCKING FRAME
911 S. Hill St. // 213-488-0373
thestockingframe.com

It's a coffee shop during the day, but starting with happy hour (5-7 p.m. at the bar) it becomes a late-night spot with cleverly concocted cocktails and sophisticated eats. Plan to run into urban hipsters seeking craft beers and deep conversation.

VOICES DOWN, DRINKS UP
LIBRARY BAR
630 W. 6th St. // 213-614-0053
librarybarla.com

When you're craving an early-evening spicy margarita, hit up this loungey, low-key spot, perfect for sophisticated cocktails and reasonably priced share plates. If not tequila, opt for a classic daiquiri, a glass of wine or a local draft beer, and enjoy the live music or Monday's DJ set.

WHEELS IN MOTION
COLE'S RED CAR BAR
118 E. 6th St. // 213-622-4090
213dthospitality.com

The restaurant may be renowned for its French Dip sandwiches, but Red Car Bar is particularly popular among Downtown denizens for its happy hour, offering classic cocktails and cheap eats from 3-7 p.m. Even better, happy hour lasts all day long on Tuesdays.

CHEAP EATS

Wurstküche

HOT DIGGITY DOG
WURSTKÜCHE
800 E. 3rd St. // 213-687-4444
wurstkuche.com

Head here when you're craving something as simple as a hot dog but complex enough to leave your taste buds wanting more. This sausage spot divides its menu into three categories: the classics ($6.50), the gourmet ($7.50) and the exotics ($8.50). How adventurous are you feeling?

PARA CHEAP COMIDA
CASA LA DOÑA
800 S. Main St. // 213-627-7441

For tasty Mexican eats that won't break the bank (tacos, burritos, you name it—it's here), head to Casa La Doña, where a salsa bar gives you nearly 20 colorful garnish options—a rainbow of spice and flavor—and Taco Tuesday means $1 tacos, from carne asada to pastor to pollo.

PAUL SUN

Pellicola Pizzeria

DIP INTO TRADITION
COLE'S
118 E. 6th St. // 213-622-4090
213dthospitality.com

Travel back in time to this traditional saloon for French Dip sandwiches and classic cocktails. For the real deal, you'll want to stop in on Tuesdays, when happy hour lasts all day and you can order half a French Dip and fries for only $5.

AN L.A. LANDMARK
PHILIPPE, THE ORIGINAL
1001 Alameda St. // 213-628-3781
philippes.com

One of two historic spots Downtown to grab a French Dip, the cafeteria line at this 1908 Chinatown institution serves up nothing but old-school deli favorites. And more than the restaurant's communal digs, the prices here are a bit nostalgic, too.

PIZZA

FAR FROM PRICEY
FAR BAR
347 E. 1st St. // 213-617-9990
farbarla.com

Practically hidden in Little Tokyo (you'll need to keep an eye open for its narrow alleyway entrance), Far Bar serves up American and Asian dishes, from sushi rolls and sliders to chicken wings and fusion tacos, all for fairly cheap prices. Grab a spot on the patio and enjoy.

FASHIONABLE FALAFEL
SANTEE FALAFEL
1335 Santee St. // 213-749-2555
santeefalafel.com

This counter-service café serves up kababs, shawarma and its fried chickpea namesake to in-the-know locals on the hunt for delicious cheap eats. It's perfect for a quick bite between rounds of shopping in the Fashion District.

THE BEST OF BOTH WORLDS
PELLICOLA PIZZERIA
421 W. 8th St. // 213-614-8000
213dthospitality.com

A favorite among Downtown locals, the pies here combine the best of New York and Neapolitan pizza worlds. Even better, you can settle into the Golden Gopher next door for a couple beers and order a slice, deliverable right to your bar stool.

DOWN-HOME ITALIAN EATS
TERRONI
802 S. Spring St. // 213-221-7234
terroni.com

Yes, the rumors are true—at Terroni, you'll cut your own slices of pizza, just like you're visiting Southern Italy. Large enough to serve two or three, the pizza is crisp and thin, and you can't go wrong with the standard Margherita.

NOSH BETWEEN MOSHING
PRUFROCK PIZZERIA
446 S. Main St. // 213-284-5661
theregenttheater.com

Attached to live music hot spot The Regent Theater, Prufrock offers delicious Neapolitan-style slices. Choose from one of a dozen personal-sized pies or make your own; either way, you're gonna get fresh ingredients on a bubbly crust.

Philippe, The Original

JOE KNOWS PIZZA
JOE'S PIZZA
613 S. Spring St. // 213-988-8848
joespizza.it

A no-nonsense pizza joint, Joe's aims to bring a little New York to the West Coast, and some say it's the closest to a New York slice you'll find in L.A. Among the locals' favorites are the cheese, the grandma and the white pizzas.

HAND-TOSSED HAPPINESS
PIZZANISTA!
2019 E. 7th St. // 213-627-1430
pizzanista.com

This pizza parlor was started by former pro skateboarder Salman Agah's "New York pizza with California ingredients" mindset. It's popular among Downtown locals, not least of which due to its sourdough crust. For something different, try a Sicilian slice.

FOR A SPICY SLICE
PAPI'S PIZZERIA
109 E. 8th St. // 213-623-3588
papispizzeria.com

A great option for dining in or delivery, Papi's specializes in "straight-forward pizzas" at reasonable prices, meaning the focus of its smaller menu is on top-notch quality. Many locals are big fans of the Zapata, made with a spicy sauce, chorizo and jalapeño.

JAPANESE

Shibumi

TOFU TAKES FLIGHT
IZAKAYA GAZEN
362 E. 1st St. // 213-613-1415
e-k-c.co.jp/gazen/la

Whether you're new to Japanese food altogether or a huge fan, this is a good place to start. Between shabu shabu, izakaya menu and sushi options, you can't really go wrong. Be sure to get the tofu sampler, featuring tofu made in-house every morning.

OODLES OF UDON
MARUGAME MONZO
329 E. 1st St. // 213-346-9762

This spot, known for drawing a hip crowd, is renowned for its hand-pulled udon noodles crafted in the kitchen. (You'll watch them get made while you eat.) Opt for more traditional dishes, or slurp up more creative concoctions, like the sea urchin cream udon.

Marugame Monzo

ARTFUL PLATES
SHIBUMI
815 Hill St. // 213-265-7923
shibumidtla.com

This intimate bar and restaurant—only open for dinner—is kappo-style, which means instead of sashimi and rolls, you're served intricately plated, complex dishes (some hot, some cold, some sweet, some rice-based) on the 400-year-old cypress tree counter.

KEEPING WITH TRADITION
T.O.T. RESTAURANT
345 E. 2nd St. // 213-680-0344
littletokyorestaurant.com

Short for "Teishokuya of Tokyo," this contemporary (but still traditional) spot is popular for its rice bowls, noodle dishes, sushi and vast sake options (more than 20 labels), though many step inside for the tonkatsu (deep-fried pork cutlet). This cozy little spot is popular for lunch and dinner.

HOUSE OF 1,000 CURRIES
CURRY HOUSE
123 Astronaut E. S. Onizuka St. #204
213-620-0855 // curryhouse-usa.com

This casual California chain has served up homestyle Japanese dishes—a variety of curries, katsu and noodle dishes since the '80s, and it still draws lines out the door, especially for lunch. For a Japanese dish you likely aren't familiar with, order the menchi katsu curry.

BREAKING WITH TRADITION
IZAKAYA & BAR FU-GA
111 S. San Pedro St. // 213-625-1722
izakayafu-ga.com

It's not easy to find, but this sleek spot serves up small plates, steaks and sushi in its underground lounge. (You'll have to look for the tiny street-level sign.) Tradition is shrugged off for what is basically a Japanese take on delicious bar food and inventive fusion.

Kazunori

SUSHI & SASHIMI

GET TO COOKING
SHABU-SHABU HOUSE
127 Japanese Village Plaza Mall
213-680-3890

Nope, it's not a sauna; it's a shabu-shabu house! You'll be cooking your own meal at this local spot credited with bringing the cooking style to L.A. Meats, veggies and noodles are cooked in a hot pot tableside before they're served with rice. Just be prepared to wait for a table or counter seat.

CRAZY STUPID FRESH
SUSHI KOMASA
351 E. 2nd St. // 213-680-1792
komasasushi.com

Locals lineup at this Little Tokyo sushi den—a staple for 20 years with its 10-seater sushi bar and half a dozen tables—especially during peak hours. And for good reason, as it's hard to find fresher, better quality nigiri, sashimi and rolls than at this intimate spot.

BRING ON THE FISH
SUSHI GEN
422 E. 2nd St. // 213-617-0552
sushigen-dtla.com

Located in Honda Plaza, sushi-lovers flock here for the sashimi deluxe plate, which arrives at your table loaded with the day's freshest fish. It's a popular spot for an inexpensive lunch, too, even among some of the city's most renowned local chefs.

NEW-SCHOOL IZAKAYA
KINJIRO
424 E. 2nd St. // 213-229-8200
kinjiro-la.com

Octopus ceviche, beef tongue and the bone-marrow dengaku are but three stars of the menu at this quiet Little Tokyo spot, an artisanal izakaya that serves both traditional and new-school small plates, complemented by a nice selection of Japanese craft beers and sake.

KNOW YOUR ROLL
KAZUNORI
421 S. Main St. // 213-493-6956
kazunorisushi.com

Calling itself "The original hand roll bar," KazuNori takes pride in being a first-of-its-kind sushi spot, serving only made-to-order hand rolls of crispy nori, warm rice and the freshest of seafood. An offshoot of Sugarfish, it has the same attention to detail with a more casual vibe.

TRUST THE CHEF
SUSHI ZO
334 S. Main St. // 424-201-5576
sushizo.us

Downtown's high-end spot for a true omakase experience (you're unable to order à la carte), helmed by Osaka-born chef Keizo Seki, serves traditional sushi to true fish-lovers, and no two dining experiences will ever be the same. With sake, expect to spend at least $200 per person.

RAMEN

ALL ABOUT AUTHENTICITY
SHIN-SEN-GUMI
132 S. Central Ave. // 213-687-7108
shinsengumigroup.com

The specialty at this popular Little Tokyo spot is Hakata Ramen, known for its milky pork-bone broth and thin, non-curly noodles. (It's a favorite of world-renowned L.A. food critic Jonathan Gold.) In addition to the ramen, enjoy yakitori, sushi and even shabu-shabu.

A BOWL OF OLD-SCHOOL
HANA ICHIMONME
333 Alameda St., Ste. 303
213-626-3514

A casual third-floor spot offering up curries, noodle soups and bento boxes in addition to its ramen, Hana Ichimonme offers reasonably priced bowls, served with complimentary iced green tea. It's also known for its wide-ranging selection of authentic Japanese sweets.

MAN OH MAN
MEN-OH TOKUSHIMA RAMEN
456 E. 2nd St. // 213-687-8485
menohusa.com

This regional chain of ramen joints has put itself on the map with its homemade broths and noodles, serving a Tokushima-style of ramen (a region famous for its pork) garnished with stir-fried strips of pork belly. It's also well-loved for its Japanese fried chicken, karaage.

ALL FOR YOU
MY RAMEN BAR
321 ¼ E. 1st St. // 213-613-9888

Most who make it into My Ramen Bar (formerly called Manichi Ramen), one of Japan's most well-known spots for ramen and also popular in Hawaii), opt for the #1 Manichi Special—tonkotsu ramen, served in a traditional bright red ceramic bowl. And don't pass up the renowned gyoza dumplings.

Men-Oh Tokushima Ramen

VEGETARIAN / VEGAN

TOTAL BODY NOURISHMENT
CAFE GRATITUDE
300 S. Santa Fe Ave. // 213-929-5580
cafegratitude.com

This local SoCal chain serves nothing but organic, plant-based food and seeks to promote consciousness and sustainability, which it does through solidly crafted salads, sandwiches, wraps and warm entrées. A favorite spot among local veggies.

MODERN VEGGIE EATS
ZINC CAFE & MARKET
580 Mateo St. // 213-825-5381
zinccafe.com

Serving up vegetarian takes on American comfort food (pizzas, burgers, sandwiches), the courtyard of Zinc is a much-needed respite from the industrial streets of the Arts District, as is the sleek, modern indoor dining room. Mixology lounge Bar Mateo sits out back.

RAW EATS
AU LAC
710 W. 1st St. // 213-617-2533
aulac.com

Serene is how most people describe the dining room of this vegan Vietnamese spot, specializing in plant-based dishes that are flavorful and use only the freshest ingredients. It's been in the L.A. area for nearly a decade, a leader in the local raw food movement.

FOR A VEGAN SLICE
PIZZANISTA!
2019 E. 7th St. // 213-627-1430
pizzanista.com

Former pro skateboarder Salman Agah lures in vegan Downtown dwellers along with meat-lovers at his beloved local parlor. Thanks to his vegan cheeses, vegan pepperoni and vegan mac 'n' cheese, everything on the menu can be ordered animal product-free.

PALTROW-APPROVED
THE SPRINGS
608 Mateo St. // 213-223-6226
thespringsla.com

If there were a holistic heaven, this would be it. The wellness center and café is 13,500 square feet of organic cold-pressed juice, vegan dining, yoga and natural health services. For wellness junkies, it's green living at its finest.

BE A LITTLE BAD
LOCALITA & THE BADAASSERIE
817 S. Los Angeles St. // 213-623-3223
localiyours.com

With the slogan "Vegan food that tastes like it isn't," this hole-in-the-wall spot is proud to be 100% plant-based, serving up healthy and hearty bites like its popular "Badass" breakfast sandwich, vegan chili and quinoa bowls.

SUSHI DONE DIFFERENTLY
SHOJIN
333 S. Alameda St., Ste. 310 // 213-617-0305
theshojin.com

This upscale vegan and macrobiotic Japanese spot holds its customers' health in the highest regard, which is why it replaces the fish you'd normally find in rolls and ramen with spicy tofu.

IT'S OK TO VEG OUT
P.Y.T.
400 S. Main St. // 213-687-7015 // pytlosangeles.com

No one seems to do Downtown as well as Chef Josef Centeno. His latest creation splits Ledlow in half and puts veggies centerstage. Inspired by local vegetable farms, P.Y.T's menu features fresh, in-season produce in mouth-watering combinations sure to satisfy even the hungriest meat-eaters. (We're talking dishes like melon with coffee cake persimmon, rye crumb, reed avocado, buttermilk and strawberry butter, or the Kong's jicama and Yali pear salad with pomegranate, avocado, and lemon verbena vinaigrette.) While veggies may rule here, P.Y.T. isn't exactly what you'd call a vegetarian or vegan restaurant. You'll still find meat like uni or ribeye on the menu, along with plenty of cheese and butter. He even makes room for a few housemade pasta dishes. So run—don't walk—here for dinner. Be sure to check out their brunch menu on weekends, too. Seriously, a vegetable-based restaurant with seasonal produce *and* lots of butter? Chef Centeno really gets us. —*L.M.*

DYLAN + JENI

JUICE

GET CLEANSED
JUICE CRAFTERS
702 S. Spring St. // 213-689-4555 // juicecrafters.com

Keep your cleanse going by stopping into this juice bar, where the prices are comparatively inexpensive and only the freshest ingredients are used in its juices, smoothies and açaí bowls.

GET READY TO DETOX
PRESSED JUICERY
860 S. Los Angeles St. // 213-688-9700 // pressedjuicery.com

Geared toward those seeking cold-pressed juices for a cleanse (and those seeking out the milkshake-like almond milk concoctions), Pressed Juicery sells a variety of fresh formulas perfect for a detox.

ALIVE AND KICKING
WILD LIVING FOODS
760 S. Main St. // 213-266-8254 // wildlivingfoods.com

"Live Dirty, Eat Clean" is the slogan of this brightly colored corner space in the Fashion District. The cold pressed juices are pre-made in the kitchen and sold in glass bottles. "Gorilla Milk" (cucumber, kale, almonds, dates, green apples and pink salt) is a customer favorite. Also raw food, smoothies and dairy free gelato.

DRINK YOUR VEGGIES
PRESS BROTHERS JUICERY
317 S. Broadway // 213-389-3645
pressbrothersjuicery.com

This juice stand inside Grand Central Market wants to replenish your body through fresh juices, cleanses and even cold-pressed popsicles. Enjoy its juices with your meal or as a meal.

GRANT KOMJAKRAPHAN

That Loose Leaf Life
AMERICAN TEA ROOM
909 S. Santa Fe Ave. // 213-239-9100 // americantearoom.com

This urban sanctuary is the stuff tea lovers' dreams are made of. Located in the Arts District near Bestia and Stumptown, this block seems to have all your food and beverage needs covered. Featuring 5,600 square feet of tea, tea-infused drinks, teaware and pastries from Valerie Confections, the high ceilings and minimalist décor are both welcoming and elegant. There's plenty of comfortable seating indoors and on the outdoor patio, whether you're looking to perch with your laptop or enjoy a hipster tea party. The best part–drinks are as delicious as they are Instagram-worthy. *–L.M.*

OUR FAVES
EAT
DTLA
DISTRICT BOOK

SWEET TOOTH

PEDAL TO THE METAL
PEDDLER'S CREAMERY
458 S. Main St. // 213-537-0257
peddlerscreamery.com

Where else can you hop on a stationary bike and help create your local parlor's ice cream and sorbets? With a focus on sustainability, Peddler's Creamery lets you help craft its sweet treats (some of which are even vegan), and for each batch you churn, you'll get a free scoop!

COFFEE AND A SLICE
THE PIE HOLE
714 Traction Ave. // 213-537-0115
thepieholela.com

This sleek local chain serves up both sweet and savory from-scratch pies—some by the slice, some personal hand pies—to Downtown denizens looking for a tasty treat. A slice is perfectly paired with The Pie Hole's medium-roast coffee, available as espresso, drip coffee or cold brew.

DESSERT FOR DINNER
NICKEL DINER
524 S. Main St. // 213-623-8301
nickeldiner.com

On the hunt for something sweet? You can't go wrong with this creator of the maple bacon donut. All the vintage eats here are amazing, but dessert is the shining star, whether you opt for the various donuts or homemade versions of classics like Pop Tarts and Ding Dongs.

FROZEN TREATS
GELATERIA ULI
541 S. Spring St., Ste. 104 // 213-900-4717
gelateriauli.com

This Historic Core spot serves coffee, espresso and pastries in addition to its homemade gelato and sorbets, made on-site daily. Popular flavors stock the case, while a rotating roster of seasonal favorites make guest appearances when the weather is right.

GOURMET DEFINED
BOTTEGA LOUIE
700 S. Grand Ave. // 213-802-1470
bottegalouie.com

A Downtown gem, this bright and bustling space serves up pizza, pasta and other Italian dishes, but the dessert menu is reason enough to step inside. Grab something to-go from the pastry counter, where the macarons are world-famous.

Bottega Louie

Peddler's Creamery

DTLA'S CREATIVE CREAMERY
GRESESCENT ICE CREAM
850 S. Olive St. // 213-986-7379
gresescent.com

The very first location of this newfound local chain, Gresescent aims to preserve the magic memories that accompany treating yourself to a scoop of ice cream. Flavors here are creative and delectable, with a texture best described as dense and velvety.

FRESH FROM PORTLAND
SALT & STRAW
829 E. 3rd St. // 213-988-7070
saltandstraw.com

Salt & Straw is dedicated to delivering the finest quality ice creams to your taste buds. Step in for a scoop (or a pint) of the shop's classic flavors (we particularly love the Salted, Malted, Chocolate Chip Cookie Dough) or any one of several inventive, seasonal options.

FROM BEAN TO BAR
MAST BROTHERS
816 S. Santa Fe Ave. // 213-261-0757
mastbrothers.com

The beards should have tipped us off, but these two brothers from Brooklyn actually made chocolate hip. Their 6,000-square-foot facility tour offers a look behind the beautiful packaging. For $10 you'll enjoy tastings and see the process "from bean to bar."

PEDDLER'S CREAMERY: ERIC STAUDENMAIER; BOTTEGA LOUIE: POUL LANGE

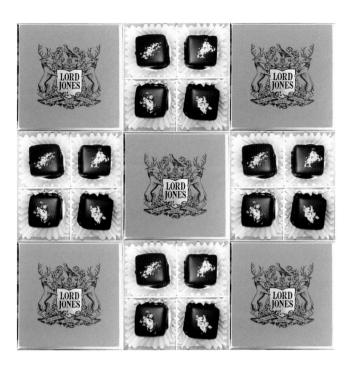

BOUTIQUE THC
LORD JONES

lordjones.com

The 2016 election was good news for pro-pot legislation in several states, including California (bringing the grand total to 28 states and Washington, D.C.). Here in California, recreational marijuana will be legal starting in 2018. What that entails exactly is still TBD, but one thing's for sure: Stoner culture is about to grow up (finally). Lord Jones is already ahead of the game as one of the first luxury cannabis product companies to come onto the scene. With gorgeous packaging and a line of handmade edibles sourced from top-quality ingredients, they take high-end dessert to the next level (or maybe some of that is the THC). Satisfy your sweet tooth with gum drops, dark chocolate sea salt caramels or dark chocolate espresso chews. And because each product comes in precise, lab-tested dosages, you'll avoid the rookie mistake of going from zero to 60 when things kick in. For those interested in the non-ingestibles, Lord Jones makes a topical moisturizing lotion, powered by Cannabidiol (CBD) and available in two strengths. CBD's topical effects are non-psychoactive and benefits range from alleviating chronic pain to reducing inflammation to soothing eczema. *—L.M.*

COFFEE SHOPS

Blue Bottle Coffee

PHIL KNOWS
PHILZ COFFEE
801 S. Hope St. // 213-213-2616
philzcoffee.com

Specializing in its own 'secret blends,' this Bay Area-based chain serves up custom blendeds (like the mint mojito iced coffee) to Downtowners needing a fix.

KYOTO-STYLE
CAFE DEMITASSE
135 S. San Pedro St. // 213-613-9300
cafedemitasse.com

A spot for coffee obsessives, this café specializes in Kyoto iced coffee (which drips for over 14 hours in a weird alchemy contraption).

MADE IN NORCAL
VERVE COFFEE ROASTERS
833 S. Spring St. // 213-455-5991
vervecoffee.com

Originated in Northern California, Verve brings international roasts to an outdoor patio in Downtown's Fashion District, and coffee aficionados can purchase home brew kits to get their fix at home.

STEP UP
G&B COFFEE at Grand Central Market
317 S. Broadway // 213-265-7718
gandb.coffee

Famed for having one of the world's best lattes, but regulars are just as intrigued by "The Business & Pleasure," a trio of tea and coffee drinks including a macadamia-almond milk latte.

SOUTHERN STYLE
BLUE BOTTLE COFFEE
582 Mateo St. // 300 S. Broadway
213-621-4194 // bluebottlecoffee.com

This newly trendy chain of caffeine outlets—selling beans and home brewing equipment along with its drinks and pastries—is beloved for its New Orleans-style iced coffee, pre-milked and sweetened.

LOCAL ROASTERS
STUMPTOWN COFFEE ROASTERS
806 S. Santa Fe Ave. // 855-711-3385
stumptowncoffee.com

This gigantic 7,000-square-foot space puts its gigantic in-house coffee roaster on display for all to see, though the real focal point at this Portland-based shop is its extensive menu.

ROCK'N BEANS
COFFEE COLAB
305 E. 8th St. Ste. 103 // coffeecolab.com

Don't be intimidated by the punk rock attitude of this local coffee shop, which uses the Japanese slow-roasting technique. You'll also find local pastries enjoyed at the sidewalk tables outside.

SIMPLE, PERIOD
BLACKTOP COFFEE
826 E. 3rd St. // 213-599-8496
blacktop.la

This tiny grab-and-go spot takes 'no frills' to heart. Order your espresso either black, white (a latte) or chocolate (a mocha), your coffee daily (the day's drip) or cold brew.

DTLA'S COFFEE CAVE
GIORGIPORGI
137 E. 3rd St. // 213-687-7753 // giorgiporgi.com

There's no coffee shop on earth quite like this one, which you'll come to realize after stepping through its moss-laden tunnel that then opens up to a very modern, minimalist coffee bar featuring little more than a concrete slab and acrylic chairs. You won't find WiFi here, because it's intended to be an Italian-style espresso bar, but what you will find is a quality cup of coffee.

DISTRICT BOOK
OUR FAVES
EAT
DTLA

TO-DIE-FOR

SEA URCHIN CREAM UDON
MARUGAME MONZO
329 E. 1st St. // 213-346-9762 // marugamemonzo.com

No one does udon better than Marugame Monzo, known for hand-pulling its noodles right there in the kitchen, and this dish, one of the restaurant's more creative concoctions, is a local favorite.

HAZELNUT PRALINE BAR
MILLA CHOCOLATES
Check website for current location // 323-515-2346 // millachocolates.com

You can't go wrong with handcrafted chocolate worthy of a glass display case. The bar is set high from the moment you enter this luxury chocolate pop-up at the Row, and lucky for us, the chocolate here is as delicious as it is beautiful, with two International Chocolate Salon awards to prove it.

PANNA COTTA
SPRING
257 S. Spring St. // 213-372-5189 // springlosangeles.com

This French restaurant has perfected its panna cotta, yet still finds ways to one-up itself. The classic dessert stays on the menu but gets a revamp depending on the fruits in-season. Past variations have included rose petal panna cotta, Tahitian vanilla panna cotta with mango, passionfruit and coconut, and panna cotta with granny smith apples and tea crumble.

Tonnarelli Alla Norcina, Terroni

TONNARELLI ALLA NORCINA
TERRONI
802 S. Spring St. // 213-221-7234 // terroni.com

Since it was added to the menu in 2015, this pasta dish has become a favorite of diners, crafted with homemade spicy sausage, pecorino, garlic and black truffle shavings. It's delizioso.

FLAKY BUTTERMILK BISCUITS
EVERSON ROYCE BAR
1936 E. 7th St. // 213-335-6166 // erbla.com

This Arts District cocktail and wine bar, featuring an expansive patio that welcomes a mix of hipsters and foodies, cranks out a ton of these flaky pastries (served with honey butter) on the daily.

CHURROS
B.S. TAQUERIA
514 W 7th St. // 213-622-3744 // bstaqueria.com

You won't find any lukewarm feelings about the churro here. Biting into one of these fluffy bad boys (only $7) is often compared to biting into a warm, soft cloud that melts in your mouth. Don't be surprised if you end up ordering more than one.

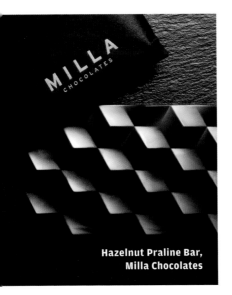

Hazelnut Praline Bar,
Milla Chocolates

Panna cotta, Spring

VRANKEN-POMMERY AMERICA
12 East 33rd Street - 7th Floor
New York, NY 10016

PLEASE DRINK RESPONSIBLY

SPEAKEASIES

PROHIBITION PARTY TIME
THE VARNISH
118 E. 6th St. // 213-265-7089
213dthospitality.com

Hidden behind iconic Downtown sandwich shop Cole's, this dark and moody spot serves up some of the city's most sophisticated old-school-era cocktails. The 1920s serve as inspiration here—for the bartenders, who are clad in suspenders; for the finely crafted daiquiris, Manhattans and gin fizzes; and for the clientele, who keep their drink-in-hand conversations hushed.

DRUNK WITH POWER
THE EDISON
108 W. 2nd St. // 213-613-0000
edisondowntown.com

This sophisticated spot was built in 1910, when it served as Downtown L.A.'s first power plant. Now the massive nightclub space invokes Art Nouveau, Steampunk and Gothic décor as one of the city's most sophisticated venues. More than a purveyor of absinthe and craft cocktails, live burlesque, music and aerialists all make their way onto the weekly calendar.

For Rooftop bars see page 22

Crane's Bar

The Varnish

A BAR TO BANK ON
CRANE'S BAR
810 S. Spring St. // 323-787-7966

Popular with regulars thanks to reasonably priced cocktails and a relaxed vibe, Crane's relies on a street-level neon sign to lead patrons into its former bank vault space. You won't be able to surf the web on your phone (or post to Instagram) while boozing it up in this basement, but you'll quickly discover that's part of this casual spot's charm. Friendly bartenders, no-frills drinks, a colorful lighting scheme and well-curated jukebox keep patrons coming back, especially for the 5-7 p.m. happy hour, which offers shot and beer specials.

ISLAND NIGHTS
CAÑA RUM BAR
714 W. Olympic Blvd. // 213-745-7090
213dthospitality.com

Featuring over 250 varieties of the sugarcane spirit, this 'members only' spot (join for $20 per year) seeks to elevate the rum-based cocktails you know and love. The bar's convivial crowd—sipping on piña coladas, daiquiris, mojitos and Caña's popular rum punch—will have you pining for the malecón of Havana.

SOUTHERN SIPS
THE LITTLE EASY BAR
216 W. 5th St. // 213-628-3113
littleeasybar.com

A maze-like pathway transports you to New Orleans' Garden District—courtesy of chandeliers, wrought iron trellises, a courtyard fountain and old-fashioned Southern hospitality. Well-crafted cocktails and authentic NOLA eats (po' boys, gumbo, beignets) make this a great spot for brunch or a late-night bite.

ONE OF A KIND

Pacific Seas at Clifton's Republic

Las Perlas

SOUTH OF THE BORDER
LAS PERLAS
107 E. 6th St. // 213-988-8355
213dthospitality.com

Popular among Downtown hipsters, the Mexican kitsch factor is high at this hotspot, where tequila and mescal are the stars of the bar shelves. Recount your cocktail cravings to the bartender for a bespoke beverage, or opt for signature libation The Spiced Daisy, a perfect blend of sweet, spicy and smoky.

THROUGH THE DRINKING GLASS
CLIFTON'S REPUBLIC
648 S. Broadway // 213-627-1673
cliftonsla.com

Reopened in 2015 following massive reconstruction, this cabinet of curiosities houses five bars in addition to its old-school food service, each with its own theme. The beer-focused, California-themed Monarch Bar sits in the dining room, while the fourth floor Pacific Seas is a pan-Pacific tiki paradise.

GEEK OUT
EIGHTYTWO
707 E. 4th Pl. // 213-626-8200
eightytwo.la

The 'barcade' concept comes alive at this Arts District hotspot, where clever mixology mixes with classic arcade games and pinball. The cocktail menu features drinks with 8-bit-inspired names, plus caffeinated options (made with local roaster LAMILL coffee) to keep your mind sharp during long bouts of Ms. Pac Man.

COSPLAY & COCKTAILS
WINE BAR C
428 E. 2nd St. // 213-628-8877
barc.biz

The most interesting aspect of this Little Tokyo bar, more than its selection of wine and sake, is that you'll be served by buxom women in French maid or geisha costumes. (The furry walls run a close second.) Be wary of signature cocktail The Galvatron, a potent concoction known to cause blackouts and loss of inhibitions.

GET YOUR PONG ON
SPIN STANDARD
550 S. Flower St. // 213-439-3065
losangeles.wearespin.com

Located in The Standard, this is L.A.'s only spot for a serious game of table tennis. Open late, the venue offers craft cocktails, a bar menu and 11 custom tables on Olympic-quality cushioned flooring. Come for casual play, partake in a tournament or take advantage of private instruction with the pros.

HISTORIC HIDEAWAY
GALLERY BAR & COGNAC ROOM
506 S. Grand Ave. // 213-624-1011

Housed in one of L.A.'s most stunning properties, the Millennium Biltmore, this ornate hotel bar is a sophisticated good time, particularly during jazz-soundtracked weekend evenings. Cozy up with one of six unique Manhattans at the Gallery Bar or get comfortable in the couch-filled Cognac Room.

KEEP IT CLASSIC
SEVEN GRAND
515 W. 7th St. // 213-614-0736
213dthospitality.com

Built to resemble a vintage hunting lodge (think Don Draper's bar of choice), the emphasis here is on a well-curated whiskey selection so massive that it requires a bar-mounted ladder. While weekend evenings can get a bit raucous, happy hour offers a mellow spot to imbibe a Manhattan or Old Fashioned.

BREWERIES

ASK THE ANGELS
ANGEL CITY BREWERY
216 Alameda St. // 213-622-1261 // angelcitybrewery.com

This beloved Arts District spot is so much more than its brewery, tap room and pub; it has become a local hub for community gatherings, from carnivals and festivals to the weekly farmers market hosted in the triangle lot adjacent to the brewery. Enjoy some of Angel City's most popular brews, sample a few limited and trial runs and feel free to bring in outside food for a fun time. Best of all, Angel City offers free brewery tours Thursday through Sunday. Just sign up with one of the on-site bartenders when you arrive.

SOPHISTICATION ON TAP
IRON TRIANGLE BREWING CO.
1581 Industrial St. // 310-424-1370
irontrianglebrewing.com

At 40,000 square feet, Iron Triangle is the largest of L.A.'s local breweries, and its brewing system is placed front and center to be admired. The tap room—offering 10 brews—has a sophisticated throwback vibe, echoing the 1920s with its long bar and fresh flowers. This ain't your frat brother's brewery.

BEER IS BOOMING
BOOMTOWN BREWERY
700 Jackson St. // 213-617-8497
boomtownbrew.com

More than just a brewery, Boomtown seeks to create a community space through gallery showings, block parties and live music. Every beer label has been designed by an L.A. artist, and the tap room—outfitted with foosball, darts, a pool table and more games—is designed with local furnishings and fixtures.

GAME ON!
ARTS DISTRICT BREWING CO.
828 Traction Ave. // 213-817-5321
213dthospitality.com

Producing 3,300 barrels of craft beer every year, here you're free to enjoy nearly 20 brews in the spacious main room or on the outdoor patio, in between games of ping-pong, darts and—best of all—vintage Skeeball. Hit up the take-out window for bar snacks that pair perfectly with stouts and IPAs.

DON'T TAP OUT
MUMFORD BREWING CO.
416 Boyd St.
mumfordbrewing.com

One of the latest breweries to hit the Downtown scene, at any given time Mumford offers up a dozen beers on tap, including IPAs, porters and pale ales. The only food you'll find on-site are freshly baked pretzels, so bring food with you, and when you find a brew you like, have some canned to enjoy at home.

Angel City Brewery

JOHN HOUCK

Garçon de Café

WINE BARS

DRINK & SHOP
GARÇONS DE CAFÉ
541 S. Spring St. // 213-278-0737
garcons-de-cafe.com

Located in the Historic Core's Broadway Spring Arcade, this spot is part-wine bar, part-boutique, furnished with vintage furniture sourced from local flea markets. Between flights of unique French wine labels, browse a cleverly curated selection of fashion (men's and women's) and accessories.

DON'T BREAK
THE BANK
POUR HAUS WINE BAR
1820 Industrial St. // 213-327-0304
pourhauswinebar.com

Find your new favorite wine among this bar/ market's worldly selection, and when you find a label you like, purchase a few bottles to take home. Known for hosting one of Downtown's best happy hours, Pour Haus offers an extensive selection of light bites in addition to vino and local craft beers.

RELAXED & RUSTIC
MIGNON
128 E. 6th St. // 213-489-0131
mignonla.com

This French bistro pours a rotating selection of around 30 small-production European wines—all of which are available for purchase by the bottle—and serves classic French plates. An intimate spot offering fewer than 20 seats, stop in for happy hour or the three-course, prix-fixe dinner, which makes for a romantic night out.

A ROCKIN'
WINE BAR
BOTTLEROCK L.A.
1050 S. Flower St. // 213-747-1100
bottlerockla.com

Delve through more than 800 wine labels, many from top producers, in addition to craft beers from around the world (18 on tap) and an eclectic menu of small bites and entrées. Stop in before a game or concert at the nearby L.A. Live, and order just two glasses for them to open any bottle you like.

NEIGHBORHOOD BARS

SIMPLE SOPHISTICATION
EVERSON ROYCE BAR
1936 E. 7th St. // 213-335-6166 // erbla.com

Head through E.R.B.'s orange door for a welcoming night of cocktails, great eats and casual conversation. Its Arts District location guarantees a hip if not slightly older crowd, and the cocktail program—best enjoyed on the spacious back patio with the bar's comfort food options—is truly inspired.

Everson Royce Bar

SO FAR, SO GOOD
FAR BAR
347 E. 1st St. // 213-617-9990
farbarla.com

A favorite spot among beer aficionados, this easy-to-miss Little Tokyo bar (keep your eyes peeled for its narrow entrance) has over 30 selections on tap, and that's in addition to its hundreds of whiskeys, many of which are stateside rarities. Head to the twinkling patio for inspired, Asian-influenced eats.

DO THE DIP
COLE'S RED CAR BAR
118 E. 6th St. // 213-622-4090
213dthospitality.com

This famed French Dip restaurant has been a cherished landmark since 1908, and when you step up to Red Car's 40-foot bar, you'll feel like you've stepped back in time. Recalling its own early years with penny-tiled floors and historic photos, the cocktails here—classic but creative, and changing with the seasons—are timeless.

ROCK AROUND THE BAR
WENDELL
656 S. Main St. // 213-622-7200
wendellbardtla.com

Named for Wendell Green, who opened some of the city's most legendary bars, the motto of this two-story space is "keep it simple." The beer selection ranges from local drafts to cans of PBR (you won't find bottles here), which pairs nicely with a hot dog and the rock-filled old-school jukebox.

GET SLOSHED IN STYLE
PATTERN BAR
100 W. 9th St. // 213-627-7774
patternbar.com

Located in Downtown's Fashion District (hence the name), here's a bar that's as stylish as its patrons. The black-and-white décor is simple and sleek, with gigantic windows that make it a great place to drink and be seen. Keeping with the bar's fashionable theme, the cocktails are named after fashion's finest.

DYLAN + JENI

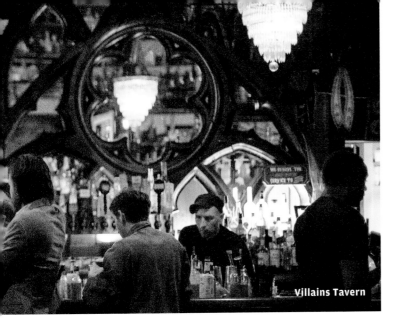

Villains Tavern

MAKE MUSICAL MEMORIES
THE LOVE SONG BAR
446 S. Main St. // 323-284-5728
theregenttheater.com

A cozy spot connected to the Regent Theater, it's a great choice whether you're concert pre-gaming or craving a civilized cocktail, while the crowd largely depends on the next-door headliner. Enjoy old-school music from a record player while ordering drinks named after your favorite rockers.

NO JOKE DRINKS
PRANK
1100 S. Hope St. // 213-493-4786
prankbar.com

An open-air, walk-up bar in South Park known for its inventive pairings, imperfect mischief and bitchin music is a bar we can get on board with. At the helm is Dave Whitton, the guy behind Villain's Tavern. Between that and the vegan nachos, things are off to a promising start for Prank.

NO RUSH, NO FUSS
TONY'S SALOON
2017 E. 7th St. // 213-622-5523
213dthospitality.com

Check the chalkboards inside for an extensive list of mescal and other spirits on-hand at this dark dive bar, formerly a hangout of hipster hero Hunter S. Thompson. Shoot pool, enjoy the jukebox, throw some darts or play ping-pong between drinks, and when you get hungry, order a slice from Pizzanista next door.

COCKTAIL CONCOCTIONS
VILLAINS TAVERN
1356 Palmetto St. // 213-613-0766
villainstavern.com

Travel off the beaten path to find this unassuming 'art bar' with an apothecary theme. There's never a cover to enjoy live music on the patio (mostly blues, rock and bluegrass), and its mixologists will whip you up something magical in a mason jar. Craft beer and delicious bites are an added bonus.

BRADLEY TUCK/NOTED MEDIA

Queen Kong at Precinct

DISTRICT BOOK **OUR FAVES**

DRINK

DTLA

LGBTQ

YOUR QUEER PARTY PALACE
PRECINCT
357 S. Broadway // 213-628-3112 // precinctdtla.com

Located in a former police precinct, this multi-room nightclub has become Downtown's go-to spot for queer lovers of drag, dancing and rock 'n' roll debauchery. The second-floor spot's wrap-around patio acts as a refuge for smokers, while the main room's stage acts as a beloved home to talented local performers, comedians and musicians.

DRINK BETWEEN THE LINES
REDLINE
131 E. 6th St. // 213-935-8391
redlinedtla.com

A sleek and modern gay bar located in the Historic Core, Redline draws boys and girls (mostly boys) with its hunky bar staff, roster of rotating DJs and regular performances by some of the city's most popular drag queens. Drinks are stiff and reasonably priced, and the patrons are a friendly bunch.

B-I-N-G-O!
DRAG QUEEN BINGO
317 S. Broadway // 213-624-2378
grandcentralmarket.com

Jeffrey Bowman, better known as "Bingo Boy," brings his cast of drag queen sidekicks to Grand Central Market every first and third Thursday of the month. It's a sassy version of the game you know and love, featuring a plethora of prizes and rather creative punishments for those who claim a false BINGO.

STACHE-TASTIC
MUSTACHE MONDAYS AT THE LASH
117 Winston St. // 213-687-7723

You may not think of Monday night as a popular one to hit the town, but this edgy underground party has been going on for years, attracting the city's drag stars, club kids and in-the-know hipsters. In addition to sets by resident DJ and founder Josh Peace, the party regularly boasts performances by queer musicians and artists.

NO-FRILLS FUN
NEW JALISCO
245 S. Main St. // 213-613-1802

The oldest of Downtown's current batch of gay bars, the New Jalisco caters to a Latin crowd with Spanish-language drag performances and Latino go-go boys, though a mix of people call this neighborhood bar home. Step into this cash-only spot for a night of cumbia, reggaeton and pop music.

FOR A CLASSY COCKTAIL
BAR MATTACHINE
221 W. 7th St. // 213-278-0471

The only gay bar in L.A. specializing in craft cocktails (with names resembling an LGBT history lesson), this gorgeously appointed two-story space draws an upscale clientele of queer folk and allies. More sophisticated and civilized than raucous, a roster of local DJs and performers call the space home.

Bar Mattachine

The Reserve

Our/Los Angeles

CLUBS

FOR MONEYMAKERS
THE RESERVE
650 S. Spring St. // 213-327-0057 // thelareserve.com

Like most of DTLA's sophisticated nightlife hot spots, this place has history: it serves up its handcrafted cocktails in the basement of a 1920s beaux-arts bank (hence the name) and welcomes night owls with its talented DJs and three bars worth of friendly staff.

SATURDAY NIGHT FEVER
HONEYCUT
819 S. Flower St. // 213-688-0888 // honeycutla.com

Known for its multicolored, light-up dance floor, this slick spot with an old-school disco vibe invites you to get your groove on but also indulge in its expansive craft cocktail program of over 50 drinks. Split into two rooms—one for drinking, one for dancing—you can choose your own adventure.

WHERE EDM IS KING
EXCHANGE L.A.
618 S. Spring St. // 213-627-8070 // exchangela.com

Located in the former L.A. Stock Exchange building, this expansive, four-level nightclub is one of Downtown's most popular venues, inviting international DJs of the highest caliber to treat its patrons to a pulsing dance floor. You'll want to dress upscale for entry.

DANCE YOUR HEART OUT
THE MAYAN
1038 S. Hill St. // 213-746-4674 // clubmayan.com

It's not everyday you come across a club with Mayan décor, but this former movie palace is one of the city's most popular venues for concerts and club nights. The Mayan offers multiple levels of fun, usually with differing music (from tropical to Top 40) on each.

DISTILLERIES

LOCAL EXPRESSION
OUR/LOS ANGELES
915 S. Santa Fe Ave. // ourvodka.com/losangeles

Our/Vodka is a global brand that's all about local flavors. With micro-distilleries in nine cities worldwide, each city's vodka has its own unique flavor and is sourced from local ingredients. For $10, you can take a tour of their modern facility in the Arts District and taste their L.A. blend at the source.

ALL IN THE FAMILY
THE SPIRIT GUILD
586 Mateo St. // 213-613-1498 // thespiritguild.com

This guild doesn't mess around when it comes to the art of distillation. Started by a family of sixth-generation farmers, it's no surprise that everything is done in-house, from fermentation to distillation to blending. Tickets are just $10 for a 45-minute tour to "ooh" and "aah" at their gorgeous facility.

SPIRIT CENTRAL
GREENBAR DISTILLERY
2459 E. 8th St. // 213-375-3668 // greenbar.biz

Perhaps the most well-known distillery tour in the area, this company has the world's largest organic, handcrafted spirits portfolio. You'll only be able to catch a tour on Saturdays ($12 per person) here, but they have plenty going on the rest of the week like cocktail classes and tastings for you to choose from.

Ham & Eggs Tavern

DIVE BARS

ALWAYS A PARTY
LA CITA BAR
336 Hill St. // 213-687-7111 // lacitabar.com

Don't come to La Cita unless you're ready to party. With more sneakers than skanky dresses, and a vast beer selection, its reputation as a Latin bar belies its truly diverse clientele, from punks and hipsters to locals on the hunt for no-frills daytime drinks. The divey spot dedicates different nights to different dance parties, so you'll want to check the calendar for what's in store, as rockabilly, punk, reggae and Latin cumbia beats all occupy spots on the roster.

DIVE RIGHT IN
HANK'S BAR
840 S. Grand Ave. // 213-623-7718

Perfect for a stiff drink with zero pretense before heading to the nearby Staples Center, this hole in the wall, attached to the lobby of the Hotel Stillwell, is the definition of a dive bar. Most packed when there's a game screening on the TV, you likely won't have a hard time finding a spot at the bar.

NEIGHBORHOOD HANG
THE DOWN & OUT BAR
501 S. Spring St. // 213-221-7595
downandoutbar.com

Open 365 days a year, you'll find whatever you're looking for here, from video games and ping-pong during 'game night' to karaoke backed by a live band. Rotating DJs spin on the weekends, with local and touring bands tearing up the venue during the week, and you're sure to find locals playing pool between pitchers of beer.

LONG LIVE THE KING
THE KING EDDY
131 E. 5th St. // 213-629-2023 // kingeddysaloon.com

One of Downtown's favorite spots for cheap drinks, light bites and a round or two of darts, this spot has been serving L.A.'s locals and visitors since 1933 (and bootlegging before that, according to the bar owners). Enjoy more than a dozen beers and a wide range of no-frills cocktails.

LIVE MUSIC

RESPECTFULLY UNREFINED
HAM & EGGS TAVERN
433 W. 8th St. // 213-891-6939 // hamandeggstavern.com

Since 2012, this intimate hole in the wall (part-beer and wine bar, part-live music setup) has been treating locals to small-scale rock concerts by local and indie bands. Drawing a crowd of regulars, it's achieved the impossible: respectable wines with a house party vibe, perfect for the aging hipster.

WALK THE PLANK
REDWOOD BAR & GRILL
316 W. 2nd St. // 213-680-2600
theredwoodbar.com

Every now and then, you just get a craving for stiff drinks in a sunken pirate ship. Full of nautical ropes, dark wooden planks and other aquatic ephemera, The Redwood offers live music every night of the week (plus a Sunday matinee performance) and pub grub that is itself worthy of stepping inside.

GET READY TO ROCK
THE REGENT THEATRE
448 S. Main St. // 323-284-5727
theregenttheater.com

What was once a theater of L.A.'s Golden Age has become the city's leading venue for indie rock and performance art. Hosting everything from movie screenings to dance parties to a monthly rock 'n' roll flea market, it's also a one-stop shop thanks to its attached vinyl-playing bar and Neapolitan pizzeria.

ALL THAT JAZZ
BLUE WHALE BAR

Weller Court, 123 Astronaut E. S. Onizuka St.
213-620-0908 // bluewhalemusic.com

This intimate jazz club and art gallery is well-loved by local L.A. music lovers for the amazing acoustics inside. Step up to the bar for small-batch bourbons, modern craft cocktails and rotating craft beers on tap, or grab a table and a bite while enjoying jam sessions courtesy of its emerging talent.

UNDER THE SEA
MRS. FISH

448 S. Hill St. // 213-873-4444
mrsfish.com

Don't let the glowing fish tank ceiling of this underground lounge distract you from the live band rocking out center stage. This multilevel spot—garishly designed with colorful vinyl couches, velvet curtains and a motorcycle encased in glass—serves up imaginative craft cocktails and utensils-not-required small plates.

FOR THE LOVE OF MUSIC
RESIDENT

428 S. Hewitt St. // 213-628-7503 // residentdtla.com

A classy but casual reprieve from the surrounding Arts District, this multi-use space is meant to recall the spirit of an Austin, Texas, neighborhood bar. Inside you'll find a live music setup (DJs and indie rock, mostly), while the outdoor beer garden uses a refurbished trailer to serve drinks and welcomes local food trucks.

TOMMII LIM

Neonderthal playing at Resident

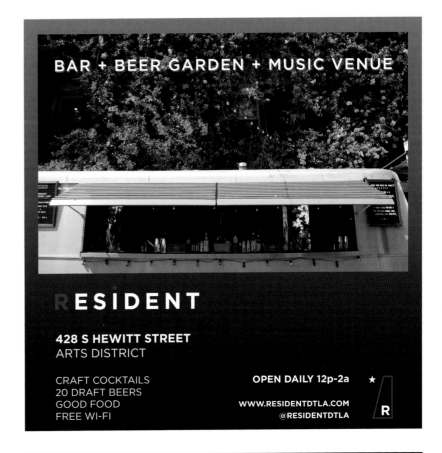

CLOTHING

Skingraft

PARISIAN FUSION
CERRE
801 Mateo St. // 323-985-8666
cerre.com

Paris-meets-California may seem like an unlikely matchup, but Cerre makes it work. Offering clean and modern styles made from luxurious materials, each piece is more than worth the investment.

BARGAINISTA
BLISS BOUTIQUE
204 ½ W. 6th St. // 213-489-4022
blissstores.com

When you need to stay on-trend but can't break the bank, it's Bliss to the rescue. With a fine selection of women's clothing, accessories and shoes starting at $30, it's no wonder this boutique has a loyal following.

CALIFORNIA COOL
ALCHEMY WORKS
826 E. 3rd St. // 323-487-1497
alchemyworks.us

A mix of retail and gallery space, this carefully curated boutique is hip to the max and includes men and women's fashion, one-of-a-kind gifts, home goods, magazines and even a Warby Parker showroom.

ON BRAND
BRIGADE LA
903 W. Olympic Blvd. //213-623-0013
brigadela.com

Marc Jacobs, Kate Spade, Furla, Jeffrey Campbell—this women's fashion retailer has all your favorite brands under one roof. Known for great sales and customer service, this location at L.A. Live is a surefire hit.

COURTESY SKINGRAFT, TANNER GOODS

DISTRICT BOOK
OUR FAVES
SHOP
DTLA

THE DARK SIDE
SKINGRAFT
758 S. Spring St. // 213-626-2662 // skingraftdesigns.com

Play with your edge as you sift the racks of this L.A.-based brand ruled by sleek designs, dark colors and fine craftsmanship. You'll feel more badass wearing this men's and women's clothing, leather goods and accessories.

LEATHER LUST
TANNER GOODS
860 S. Broadway // 213-265-7480 // tannergoods.com

If you've ever dreamed of meeting a hot lumberjack who also appreciates fine leather goods, he'd probably shop here. This Portland-based boutique is known for a top-notch selection of handcrafted leather items.

DO-GOOD FASHION
APOLIS GLOBAL
806 E. 3rd St. // 855-894-1559
apolisglobal.com

In a city where socially conscious equals sexy, this minimalist menswear boutique features shirts, swimwear, bags, outerwear and shoes, all ethically sourced. This fashion looks good on the body and feels good on the brain.

CLEAR SIGHTED
MYKITA
847 S. Broadway // 213-335-5815
mykita.com

This German brand is known for custom-fit prescription eyewear (all done in-house), with designs that straddle the line between edgy and classic. Downtown is its largest store yet and the only West Coast location.

Rich Honey

Tanner Goods

EFFORTLESSLY COMFORTABLE
RICH HONEY
210 W. 8th St. // 213-905-3205
richhoneyapparel.com

This L.A.-based apparel company takes you back to basics with locally sourced and manufactured clothing. After years in wholesale, this long-awaited retail debut includes a selection of shirts, hoodies and more.

BEACH BREAK
THE HOUSE OF WOO
209 S. Garey St. // 213-687-4800
ilovewoo.com

Nestled in the Arts District, designer Staci Woo's flagship store brings a bit of the beach to downtown. Upscale but comfortable, you'll find clothing and accessories for men, women and children, and of course beach towels.

STEP UP TO THE STREETS
NICE KICKS
862 S. Main St. // 213-542-2380
nicekicks.com

Always at the center of sneaker culture, there's never a shortage of parties, celebrities or shoe events at this online retailer's Los Angeles brick-and-mortar. Stop in and revel in the beauty of hard-to-find kicks, apparel and hats.

AUSSIE OUTPOST
BNKR
901 S. Broadway // 213-327-0442
us.fashionbunker.com

This Australian retailer's cult following spans oceans. Lucky for us, the 6,800-square-foot flagship store is the only U.S. location. You'll find women's fashion and accessories from Aussie brands like C/MEO COLLECTIVE and Jaggar Footwear.

SO SWEDE OF YOU
ACNE STUDIOS
855 S. Broadway // 213-243-0960
acnestudios.com

The opening of this sleek Swedish brand's flagship in 2013 signified a new era in DTLA. Located in the Eastern Columbia Building, its 5,000 square feet of world-famous denim, leather jackets and other minimalist must-haves await you.

BOYS CLUB
BEAUTIFUL FÜL
107 W. 5th St. // 213-614-6861
beautifulful.com

Menswear designer Alejandro Rodriguez really gets modern men, serving up classic pieces with a fresh take in this boutique at the Rosslyn Hotel. And your shopping experience comes with a fully stocked whiskey bar.

CASUAL AFFAIR
SUB_URBAN RIOT
111 W. 7th St. // 213-689-3271
suburbanriot.com

You've more than likely chuckled at someone in their signature KALE shirt, and you can expect more clever designs here. It's a lighthearted brand proudly made in the USA, and it's all about that comfy and casual life.

OOH LA LA
A.P.C.
125 W. 9th St. // 424-252-2762 // apc.fr

In good company at 9th and Broadway, this popular, ready-to-wear French brand brought a whole lot of buzz with it when it opened. Both the collections and the space itself are minimalist with très chic flair.

BONJOUR, BRO
GUERILLA ATELIER
912 E. 3rd St. // 310-365-2194
guerillaatelier.com

Blurring the lines of fashion and art, this 5,000-square-foot flagship offers a retail-meets-museum experience in the Arts District. You'll find designer fashion for men and women alike, and even furniture and home décor.

HOME / LIFESTYLE

Please Do Not Enter

WEST COAST LOVE
AS OF NOW
Moving in early 2017, location TBD
323-559-1840 // asofnowstore.com

Owners Brad Cook and Melissa Ritchie are all about spreading the love to L.A.'s local artists and designers. The curated selection of housewares, ceramics and furniture make this a great place to find locally sourced treasures.

BLADES OF GLORY
ROSS CUTLERY
324 S. Broadway // 213-626-1897
rosscutlery.com

Since 1930, this Downtown retailer has been the go-to place for all things sharp, carrying knives and blades of all kinds, as well as scissors, trimmers and flashlights. It's rumored this is where O.J. purchased a now-infamous knife—you know which one.

URBAN SOPHISTICATE
NADIA GELLER DESIGNS MARKET
1308 Factory Pl. #105 // 213-239-5655
nadiageller.com

Interior designer Nadia Geller has designed everything from commercial and residential spaces to home makeovers on Emmy-nominated TV shows. Her shop is a unique blend of custom furniture, vintage, textiles and more.

KITCHENWARE WONDERLAND
DISH FACTORY
310 S. Los Angeles St. // 213-687-9501
dishfactory.com

Whether you're on the hunt for a teacup saucer or stockpot, this restaurant-style supplier has it. The store spans 60,000 square feet—plenty of room for ramekins, frying pans and pots of all kinds.

AN UNLIKELY WARM WELCOME
PLEASE DO NOT ENTER
549 S. Olive St. // 213-263-0037
pleasedonotenter.com

Contrary to its name, this luxury retail/art exhibition space really does want you to come in and stay a while, especially design-loving men. The curated collection of design and art books, home décor and accessories is worthy of a long visit.

ALL ABOUT THAT FACE
AESOP
862 S. Broadway // 213-265-7487
aesop.com

An early pioneer of 9th and Broadway's transformation, the Australian luxury skincare brand has had a cult following since the '80s. Find plant-based skin, hair and bodycare products in a 1,000-square-foot space with a modern buildout.

STRAIGHT OUTTA PINTEREST
HAMMER AND SPEAR
255 S. Santa Fe Ave. Ste. 101
213-928-0997 // hammerandspear.com

L.A.'s interior designers rely on power couple Kristan Cunningham and Scott Jarrell for amazing vintage finds. This 5,000-square-foot showroom is a fully stocked retail mecca and interior design firm. Read more about the owners on page 66.

Nadia Geller

A TASTE OF BROOKLYN
ARTISTS & FLEAS
740 E. 3rd St. // 310-900-9987
artistsandfleas.com

This New York-based outdoor market has made its way west, popping up every first and third Saturday at the Arts District Triangle. The market features an eclectic vendor list showcasing art, design and vintage finds.

ALL AMERICAN VINTAGE
RAGGEDY THREADS
330 E. 2nd St. // 213-620-1188
raggedythreads.com

It's hard not to get nostalgic—and maybe even patriotic—in this classic Americana vintage store. From the décor to the treasure trove of shirts, shoes, overalls and dresses, you'll yearn for a simpler time, or at least want to look the part.

California Market Center
Sunglasses: YHF
Jacket: Popkiller
Dress: Goldie London

LET'S MAKE A DEAL
SANTEE ALLEY
Olympic to 12th between Maple and Santee
thesanteealley.com

With more than 150 vendors, you'll leave with your hands full after a day of shopping here. It's open daily, but weekends draw the biggest crowds. Bring cash, be prepared to bargain and pace yourself.

BEERS AND BIKES
LOT, STOCK AND BARREL
801 ½ Traction Ave. // 323-744-6774
lotstockandbarrel.com

One of L.A.'s vintage gems, the car and biker influence gives it classic edge. Grab a beer from the fridge and peruse vintage denim, jackets and tees. They even offer custom chain-stitching the old-fashioned way.

FLEA MARKET VIBES
ARTS DISTRICT CO-OP
453 Coylton St. // 213-223-6717
adcoopla.com

Head here for great flea market finds, block party-style. Lined with tasty food trucks and live music, shoppers are able to scope out handmade local goods, furniture, art, jewelry and clothing, too, all inside a funky brick building. This co-op is open every day but Monday.

GO ANOTHER ROUND
ROUND2 L.A.
600 Spring St. // 213-909-7938
round2la.bigcartel.com

A fun place to play dress-up in both modern and vintage finds—from punk rock to disco—customers rave about friendly owner Rocco and the store's vibrant, playful vibe. They offer men and women's clothing, accessories and shoes, including mind-blowing platforms.

INDIE EXPO
UNIQUE L.A.
110 E. 9th St. CMC Penthouse
uniqueusa.com

If you're hoping to shop at all your favorite Etsy stores in one place, this is it. The seasonal market has created a movement supporting small American businesses and independent designers, and it's just $10 cash to get in.

Designer Deals
CALIFORNIA MARKET CENTER
110 E. 9th St. // 213-630-3600 // californiamarketcenter.com

The showroom is off-limits to the public for tradeshows most of the time, but on the last Friday of every month, they host a sample sale. You'll know it by the line stretched around the block.

SHOPPING CENTERS

URBAN OASIS
THE BLOC
700 S. Flower St. // theblocdowntown.com

After a pricey makeover, the former Macy's Plaza is now a sophisticated, open-air spot, complete with shops (luxe brands, jewelry, toys), restaurants (a steakhouse, pizza, juice bar) and soon an Alamo Drafthouse cinema.

DOWNTOWN FUNK
THE YARDS
300 S. Santa Fe Ave // osfla.com

This 80,000-square-foot shopping center is anything but ordinary, and we wouldn't expect less in the Arts District. Part of the residential complex One Santa Fe, find brands like Wittmore, Malin+Goetz and The Voyager.

NEIGHBORHOOD WATCH
JAPANESE VILLAGE PLAZA
335 E. 2nd St. // japanesevillageplaza.net

Whether you're short on time or just looking to explore, here you'll catch a good glimpse of Little Tokyo. Between perusing boutiques filled with quirky Japanese goods and amazing dessert options, your free two-hour parking will be up in no time.

MEGA MAINSTREAM
FIGAT7TH
735 S. Figueroa St. // figat7th.com

Get all your shopping done in a flash at this downtown hub of big box stores, complete with its own weekly (Thursdays) farmer's market. It's home to City Target, Southern California's largest H&M and a 27,000-square-foot Zara flagship store.

FOODIE FANFARE
LITTLE TOKYO GALLERIA & MARKET
333 S. Alameda St.
littletokyomarket.com

Food is the name of the game at this indoor marketplace, with a good mix of Japanese and Korean options. Stop in for a hot meal or stock up on Asian pantry staples, housewares and Hello Kitty gifts you didn't know you needed.

LITTLE TOKYO

OFFBEAT FASHION
POPKILLER SECOND
300 E. 2nd St. // 213-625-1372
popkiller.us

You can't go to Little Tokyo and not stop here. Known for its unique selection of cheeky T-shirts and funky accessories, everyone leaves this edgy boutique feeling a little more hip than they were before.

BUILD IT AND THEY WILL COME
ANZEN HARDWARE
309 E. 1st St. // 213-628-2068

The friendly owner of this last remaining hardware store in Little Tokyo has been selling quality knives, gardening supplies, carpentry tools and more since 1946. Stop in for any home improvement project needs.

BOOKWORM HIDEOUT
KINOKUNIYA BOOKSTORE
Weller Court, 123 Astronaut E. S. Onizuka St.
213-687-4480 // usa.kinokuniya.com

More than just a big, beautiful bookstore, this spot has long been a pillar in L.A.'s Japanese-American community. Find a great selection of Japanese fashion magazines, manga and plenty of great reads in English as well.

HELLO KITTY HEAVEN
SANRIO
115 Japanese Village Plaza
213-687-8640 // sanrio.com

Little Tokyo wouldn't be complete without its own Sanrio store. Here you'll find a full lineup of Hello Kitty merchandise, from toys to makeup to backpacks. Don't be surprised if you also end up taking home one of her cute friends.

SNEAKERHEADS UNITE
RIF
334A E. 2nd St. // 213-617-0252
riflosangeles.com

One of L.A.'s most reputable sneaker consignment stores, this DTLA gem has been curating rare and hard-to-find kicks and clothing since 2006. The novelty comes with a hefty price tag, of course, but you can't beat the selection.

A costly rare find: Nike Lebron 11 Premium 2K14, $700 at RIF

KEEPING IT CLASSY
RAFU BUSSAN
414 E. 2nd St. // 213-614-1181
rafubussaninc.com

If you're in need of a grown-up gift, look no further than the largest gift shop in Little Tokyo. The 7,000-square-foot space offers plenty of gorgeous tea sets, ceramics, Japanese dolls, lanterns and more to choose from.

Fabrics on sale at $3-$6 per yard at Michael Levine

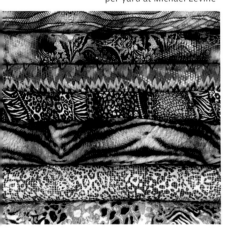

FABRIC & CRAFTS

ROLLS ON ROLLS ON ROLLS
MICHAEL LEVINE
920 S. Maple Ave. // 213-622-6259
mlfabric.com

At the "Disneyland of fabric stores," newbies and novices alike will enjoy weaving up and down the aisles of colorful fabrics to find just what they need. Prices are affordable, and the staff is happy to help.

YOU CRAFTY MINX
MOSKATELS / MICHAEL'S
733 S. San Julian St. // 213-689-4830

It's like Costco for crafters and party planners, complete with a warehouse of ribbon, frames, art supplies and everything you need for a DIY wedding. The theme changes periodically according to the season, which means you'll rarely see the same store twice.

Daiso

DOLLAR DEALS
DAISO
333 S. Alameda St. #114 // 213-265-7821 // daisojapan.com

Move over, Dollar Tree, because for $1.50 you'll find an assortment of household items, beauty supplies, gifts and more. You never know what you'll find each time you go, but the overload of cuteness is guaranteed.

TOO MANY KAWAII
TOKYO JAPANESE OUTLET
114 Japanese Village Plaza Mall
tokyojlsusa.com

If cute is what you seek, you've come to the right place. There's no shortage of adorable gifts, kitchenware, stationary and collectibles. Stock up without feeling guilty since the prices are as affordable as the selection is adorable.

BEAUTY ON A BUDGET
MAKE ASOBI
130 Japanese Village Plaza
213-620-0181

Long before Asian skincare products were all the rage, Angelenos were coming here for affordable beauty supplies. Fully stocked with Asian brands, it's impossible to leave this shop empty-handed.

Feel-Good Goods
MADE BY DWC CAFÉ AND GIFT BOUTIQUE
438 S. San Pedro St. // 213-213-2881 // madebydwc.org

Imagine if you could help provide housing for women in the Skid Row/DTLA community just by walking into a café and enjoying an organic coffee and pastry, or by shopping for a vintage handbag or an über-crafty, upcycled teacup candle made with hand-poured soy wax and essential oils. You can in DTLA, thanks to MADE by DWC Café and Gift Boutique and MADE by DWC Resale Boutique, two must-visit innovative social enterprises and stores created by the Downtown Women's Center.

Since 1978 the Downtown Women's Center has been serving women by providing supportive housing and a safe and healthy community. DWC's unique handmade products—sold at both locations and online—are made onsite by the women of DWC, inspired by product design workshops held by volunteer community artists and DWC staff. Both the workshops and the on-the-job training opportunities offered by the brick-and-mortar locations help the women develop new skills and restore self-esteem, empowering them to re-enter the workforce. "MADE by DWC allows them the space to really work through some of the barriers they've been facing living in poverty or living in homelessness," says Dena Younkin, product and merchandise senior manager. Proceeds support the DWC and its programs, including a day center, 119 permanent supportive housing units and a women's health clinic. —*Jolia Allen*

BOOKS / GIFTS / PETS

The Good Liver

DISTRICT BOOK
OUR FAVES
SHOP
DTLA

NOT-SO-GENERAL STORE
THE GOOD LIVER
705 Mateo St. // 213-947-3141 // good-liver.com

This gift boutique is all about carrying artisanal home and personal items with history and fine craftsmanship. Need an adjustable brass pencil sharpener? Or $153 hand-carved wooden bowl? You might after you walk in.

A FEAST FOR THE EYES
HENNESSEY + INGALLS
300 S. Santa Fe, Ste. M
213-437-2130 // hennesseyingalls.com

After more than two decades in Santa Monica, this well-known visual arts bookstore made the move east to the Arts District at One Santa Fe. The shelves are packed with gorgeous books on art, design and architecture.

COVER TO COVER
THE LAST BOOK STORE
453 S. Spring St. // 213-488-0599
lastbookstorela.com

A true L.A. icon, this indie bookstore is home to that infamous book tunnel you've seen on Instagram. You'll find books old and new, and they even have a music section where you can thumb through old vinyl. See page 84 for more.

THAT LIT LIFE
THE LIBRARY STORE
630 W. 5th St. // 213-228-7500
shop.lfla.org

With all sales supporting the L.A. Public Library, it takes a lot of restraint not to buy every book in the store. This carefully curated selection of literary gifts also includes toys, stationary, notebooks and more.

MADE FOR EACH OTHER
THE WHEELHOUSE
1375 E. 6th St., Unit 6 // 213-628-3117
thewheelhouse.bike

If there's one thing urban hipsters love more than their bicycles, it's a good cup o' joe. The two come together at this cycling-themed coffee shop where you can also shop or get your bike serviced.

GET CREATIVE
POKETO
820 E. 3rd St. // 213-537-0751 // poketo.com

Artsy but organized is the vibe at this Arts District staple, with everything from one-of-a-kind planters and books to wallets and backpacks with a colorful minimalist spin. They also offer a variety of creative workshops in-store.

PAMPERED PAWSIBILITIES
PUSSY & POOCH
564 S. Main St. // 213-438-0900
pussyandpooch.com

Cats and dogs are more than family here—they're almost royalty. This location features a "Pawbar" cafe where your four-legged baby can choose from raw, stews or a made-to-order dining option. Now that's luxe living.

REAL OLD SCHOOL
CARAVAN BOOKS
550 S. Grand Ave. // 213-626-9944

This rare and antique bookstore is old and musty, just the way we like it. The interior is more like an old library, the kind modern-day book worms would only dream of time traveling to. New books aren't a thing here, and neither are websites.

Poketo Store

The Broad

MUSEUMS

THE BROAD
221 S. Grand Ave. // 213-232-6200
thebroad.org

This gorgeous contemporary art museum pops with life, with close to 2,000 pieces on display from the Broad Art Foundation and the Broad family's personal collection. It's free, but reserve your spot ahead of time.

AFRICAN-AMERICAN FIREFIGHTER MUSEUM
1401 S. Central Ave. // 213-744-1730
aaffmuseum.org

L.A. is lucky to have the country's first and only African-American firefighter museum. Housed in Fire Station 30, established in 1913, you'll see a vintage fire apparatus, old photos, memorabilia and more.

FIDM MUSEUM AND GALLERIES
919 S. Grand Ave., Ste 250 // 800-624-1200
fidmmuseum.org

If you ever wanted to take a tour of all things glitz and glamour, this would be it. We're talking more than 12,000 costumes, accessories and textiles from as far back as the 18th century on permanent display.

CHINESE-AMERICAN MUSEUM
425 N. Los Angeles St. // 213-485-8567
camla.org

Located in the Garner Building, the oldest surviving Chinese building in SoCal, visitors will find everything from audio recordings to antiques to wedding gowns, located in the El Pueblo de Los Angeles.

EL PUEBLO DE LOS ANGELES HISTORICAL MONUMENT
125 Paseo de la Plaza // 213-485-6855
elpueblo.lacity.org

You could spend all day here, and plenty of people do. This monument consists of 27 historic buildings, four of which are museums. Be sure to check out the open-air marketplace on Olvera Street for food and shopping.

FIDM'S ANNETTE GREEN FRAGRANCE ARCHIVE
919 S. Grand Ave., 2nd floor // 800-624-1200
fidmmuseum.org

Another L.A. exclusive, it's the country's only perfume museum. The collection features more then 2,000 pieces of perfume pieces dating back to the late 1800s, including bottles and old advertisements.

GRAMMY MUSEUM
800 W. Olympic Blvd. // 213-765-6800
grammymuseum.org

It's more than pop culture mania at this music museum. Spanning four floors, you'll find exhibits dedicated to the influence and history of music through film and interactive experiences in almost every genre.

LA PLAZA DE CULTURA Y ARTES
501 N. Main St. // 213-542-6200
lapca.org

Located at the southern end of historic Olvera Street, this museum is the nation's premiere center of Mexican American culture and features interactive exhibits, classes, films and more.

MUSEUM OF CONTEMPORARY ART, GRAND AVENUE
250 S. Grand Ave. // 213-626-6222
moca.org

With more than 5,000 pieces collected, MOCA is a force to be reckoned with in the contemporary art scene. There's never a dull moment in the program schedule, and it's quite the hub for summer fun.

MUSEUM OF CONTEMPORARY ART, THE GEFFEN CONTEMPORARY
152 N. Central Ave. // 213-625-4390
moca.org

A hipster favorite for its industrial setting, this second MOCA location in Little Tokyo features a rotation of contemporary exhibitions and events. There's even a Pancake Epidemic Coffee Bar outside serving Stumptown coffee.

JAPANESE-AMERICAN NATIONAL MUSEUM
100 N. Central Ave. // 213-625-0414
janm.org

The beating heart of Little Tokyo, it's the country's only museum dedicated to the history of Japanese-Americans. It's the same museum that brought us a Hello Kitty exhibit, so check the calendar often for fun events year-round.

POUL LANGE

DISTRICT BOOK
OUR FAVES

DO

DTLA

SO THEATRICAL
LOS ANGELES THEATRE CENTER
514 S. Spring St. // 213-489-0994
thelatc.org

You might not guess from the outside, but this building houses several small theaters. Operated by the Latino Theater Company, the wide range of programs includes theater, international dance festivals, comedy and spoken word.

CRAFTY & CONTEMPORARY
REDCAT
631 W. 2nd St. // 213-237-2800
redcat.org

Located inside the Walt Disney Concert Hall, REDCAT isn't what you'd expect. From cutting edge architecture to innovative programs and performance art, this 200-250 capacity theater appeals to a lively, artistic crowd, but the lounge/bar appeals to all.

PERFORMANCE THEATERS

AIN'T IT GRAND
WALT DISNEY CONCERT HALL
111 S. Grand Ave // 323-850-2000
laphil.com

Home to world-class music and most notably the L.A. Philharmonic, this concert hall is as much an icon as a local favorite. Designed by the renowned Frank Gehry, catch a free tour and see the ins and outs of this grand structure.

BROADWAY MAGNET
AHMANSON THEATRE
135 N. Grand Ave. // 213-628-2772
centertheatregroup.org

Amelie, *Jersey Boys*, Rodgers and Hammerstein's *Cinderella*—there's a reason this theater has the largest theatrical subscription base on this coast. It seats 2,000, making it the perfect venue for performances of all kinds.

NOT YOUR GRANDMA'S OPERA
DOROTHY CHANDLER PAVILLION
135 N. Grand Ave. // 213-628-2772
laopera.org

This venue checks all the boxes of a grand opera house. Built in 1964, its incredible acoustics are only matched by its gigantic crystal chandeliers and classic décor. Patrons love that it has one of the largest stages in the country.

TAKE A SEAT
MARK TAPER FORUM
135 N. Grand Ave. // 213-628-2772
centertheatregroup.org

There's not a bad seat in the house at this award-winning theater, thanks to its half-circle shape. It's one of three theaters at the Music Center, so the location can't be beat. Come for plays, live music and adventurous programming.

Walt Disney Concert Hall

TOURS / ART WALK

BLAST FROM THE PAST
LOS ANGELES CONSERVANCY
523 W. 6th St., Ste. 826 // 213-623-2489 // laconservancy.org

In a city with an ever-changing skyline, this influential nonprofit organization has been a champion for historical preservation of Los Angeles for decades. As part of its work, there's a wide selection of walking tours, mostly centered on Downtown, priced at $15. **The Historic Downtown Walking Tour** starts at Pershing Square and showcases historical and cultural landmarks downtown, including the Central Library and Grand Central Market. There's also the **Art Deco Tour** where participants can appreciate the fine architecture of buildings from the 1920s and '30s, with stops at the Eastern Columbia Building and the Title Guarantee & Trust Building. And for those who love historic theaters, the **Broadway Historic Theatre** and **Commercial District Tour** focuses on the evolution of Broadway. If you're lucky, you'll get to see a few theaters from the inside.

A TALE OF TWO CITIES
DOWNTOWN L.A. WALKING TOURS
213-399-3820 // dtlawalkingtours.com

Formed in 2009, this company saw a growing interest in learning about Downtown Los Angeles, and an influx of tourists and new residents became all the more reason to share the rich history of these changing neighborhoods. **The Old & New Downtown L.A. Tour** focuses on the past and the present, while **L.A.'s Beginnings** looks back at the history that helped shape our modern day city. For TV and film buffs, the **Hollywood in Downtown L.A. Tour** heads to the filming locations of many popular movies. Tours are priced at $17.

BOOZE MEETS GRAFFITI
L.A. ART TOURS
670 Moulton Ave. #9A // 310-503-2365 // laarttours.com

For more modern-day enjoyment of all the fun things Downtown L.A. has to offer, there's L.A. Art Tours. They paired up with SoCal Brew Bus for their **Urban Art and Craft Beer Tour** ($80), which is exactly what it sounds like, covering three craft breweries, graffiti and murals all in the blossoming Arts District. If beer flights aren't your thing, the **Downtown L.A. Graffiti/Mural Tour** ($17) is led by actual DTLA muralists and artists who take you through the Arts District on foot to see completed pieces as well as artists at work.

FOOD FOR THOUGHT
AVITAL TOURS
213-394-0901 // avitaltours.com

Whether you're visiting or have lived here your entire life, this tour company wants you to love Downtown L.A. as much as they do. For $76, your walking adventure includes four courses chosen by a tour guide who also knows the ins and outs of Downtown's history.

HOW THE LOCALS DO IT
SIX TASTE
213-798-4749 // sixtaste.com

Eat like a local with this L.A.-born-and-raised, family-owned tour company. Of the nine tours offered, three are Downtown, including Little Tokyo and the Arts District. For $65-$70, you'll stop at five to six eateries and the tour can last up to four hours.

ARTSY BLOCK PARTY
DOWNTOWN ART WALK
Main and Spring between 2nd and 9th
downtownartwalk.org

This monthly event has filled streets and sidewalks with art-lovers since 2004 on the second Thursday of every month. With more than 50 galleries participating, you can either go with a game plan or just wander around.

FAR EAST EXPLORATION
CHINATOWN GALLERIES
Chung King Road in West Plaza
949 N. Hill St. // chinatownla.com

"Chinatown Art Night" is a quarterly evening event on the walkable Chung King Road. Visitors weave up and down the alleys, and it's a good way to explore a pocket of Chinatown and discover galleries at the same time.

SECRET GARDEN
BLUE RIBBON GARDEN AT DISNEY CONCERT HALL
111 S. Grand Ave. // 213-850-2000 // laphil.com

Talk about hidden gems in Los Angeles, this one is a total sanctuary that's easy to miss because it's not visible from street level. Tucked away upstairs at Disney Concert Hall is a beautifully landscaped garden, a peaceful hideaway from the hustle and bustle of city life down below. Best of all? It's free. Visitors can take a self-guided tour or sign up for a complimentary guided tour. Check out the tour schedule on their website.

TREASURE TROVE
CENTRAL LIBRARY TOUR
630 W. 5th St. // 213-228-7000 // lapl.org

One of Downtown's most prized historic buildings, the Central Library is not to be missed. Lucky for all of us, there are plenty of free opportunities to marvel at the architecture of the Tom Bradley Wing, designed by Norman Pfeiffer, or "ooh" and "aah" at the gorgeous chandeliers. Catch a free daily docent-led tour for an in-depth, personal experience, although free walk-in tours (no reservation required) are offered on certain days.

Shepard Fairey mural near East 3rd Street and Traction Avenue.

POUL LANGE

CONTRIBUTORS

Photographer **ALLEN DANIEL** was born in San Francisco, moved to Sacramento at age seven and has been based in L.A.'s Chinatown since 2016. He recently joined DJ Jackal on tour in India and photographed DJs Morgan Page and Dr. Fresch at Insomniac's Countdown New Year's Eve 2016. Daniel is currently working on "Day by Day," an ongoing series of images he takes daily and posts to his website. For the launch issue of *DISTRICT BOOK//DTLA*, Daniel photographed the fashion trendsetters of the piece "Style Squad."

See pages 30, 80

ELIZABETH TURNER is a Los Angeles–based freelance writer and editor specializing in food, culture and design. The great-granddaughter of Spanish immigrants who settled in Downtown Los Angeles in the early 20th century, she never tires of exploring the colorful streets and historic buildings of DTLA.

See pages 6, 48, 60

BEKAH WRIGHT's articles have appeared in myriad outlets from *Los Angeles* magazine and *Bon Appétit* to *TV Guide* and the *Los Angeles Times*. Beyond writing about travel and entertainment, she's the founder of Change Your Life Travels VR. Where she's determined Harry Potter really lives (and as a result is always there searching): DTLA's The Last Bookstore.

See pages 26, 70

EMI ROSE KITAWAKI's experience in running social media accounts for designer Ann Tan led to discovering her own passion for photography, which allows her to show "beauty of the moment," as she puts it. With Downtown's growth came the demand for creative content, and Kitawaki and her husband, Maurice, specialize in producing videos, social media and branding for DTLA-based businesses. The multi-talented Kitawaki is also featured as the model in "Street Cycle" and "Urban Hike."

See pages 86, 90, 136, 146

IAN SPANIER began taking photographs at six years old when his parents gave him his first point-and-shoot camera. After majoring in photography in college, Spanier worked in publishing as a photo editor, but the desire to make pictures never left him. Having only known 35mm, he taught himself medium and large format as well as lighting. His clients include Comedy Central, A&E and HBO, among others, and his book project, *Local Heroes: America's Volunteer Firefighters*, came out to critical acclaim in the fall of 2012. Although he works anywhere and everywhere, Spanier recently left New York for the sunny coast, and now lives with his wife and two sons in Los Angeles.

See page 86, 90

SHELLEY LEVITT is a transplanted New Yorker who came to Los Angeles for a three-month stint for *People* magazine 20 years ago and never left. She writes about food and travel, health and wellness, beauty and business for a wide range of publications and websites. "When I start feeling homesick, I head down to the Grand Central Market," she says. "The buzz, the mix of old and new, and the friendly jostle of the crowds feel familiar in a way that's deeply restorative. But even on the streets of my old neighborhood, you couldn't find lox, pupusas, ceviche and Texas BBQ all within footsteps of each other."

See pages 22, 42, 44

Born in L.A. and raised by the beach, photographer **JOSHUA SPENCER** shoots portraits, fashion and video. "Most of my favorite photographers are from the early Magnum days, Henri Cartier-Bresson being top of the list. There is a timeless quality to black-and-white imagery, the feeling of not knowing when the image was taken. My goal is to tell stories, be it with video or stills," he says. Spencer has recently done work for The Well X Mondrian, and a book of his portraits has been published by Garrett Leight California Optical to celebrate the company's five-year anniversary.

See page 60

DISTRICT BOOK // DTLA

KAYOKO SUZUKI-LANGE
Co-Founder & Chief Creative Officer
kayoko@district8media.com

KATHY NENNEKER
Consulting Editor

STEPHAN HORBELT
Editor

LAUREN SCHUMACHER
Photo Editor

MELISSA BRANDZEL
Copy Editor

TAJINDER REHAL
Fact Checker

SHANA WONG SOLARES
Co-Founder & Publisher
shana@district8media.com

LEIMOMI COLORETTI
Business Development Manager

AL FAER / THE JARED COMPANY
Publishing Consultant

HAL BASTIAN
Downtown Revitalization Consultant

SPECIAL THANKS TO:
Maximilian Rivera, Marko Prelic, Alexander Laurent, Gabor Ekecs, Mark Esguerra and Maiko Naito for photography; Chris Sharp and Christina Sun for map illustrations; Lydia Mack for fave list writing; Ariana Nussdorf for talent referrals; David Crowley for financial analysis; Yoko Kawaguchi for business counseling; Poul Lange, Richard Solares and our families for their unconditional support.

PUBLISHER'S NOTE:
While every effort was made to ensure accuracy at the time of publication, it is always best to call ahead and confirm that the information is up to date.

DISTRICT 8 MEDIA, LLC
315 E. 8th St., Ste. 702
Los Angeles, CA 90014
info@district8media.com
district8media.com

ADVERTISING
sales@district8media.com
808-386-0872